A WALK ON THE WEST SIDE
California on the Brink

BOOKS BY HERBERT GOLD

NOVELS

Birth of a Hero
The Prospect Before Us
The Man Who Was Not With It
The Optimist
Therefore Be Bold
Salt
Fathers
The Great American Jackpot
Swiftie the Magician
Waiting for Cordelia
Slave Trade
He/She

STORIES AND ESSAYS

Love and Like
The Age of Happy Problems
The Magic Will
A Walk on the West Side—California on the Brink

MEMOIR

My Last Two Thousand Years

A WALK ON THE WEST SIDE
California on the Brink

Herbert Gold

ARBOR HOUSE

New York

Copyright © 1981 by Herbert Gold

All rights reserved, including the right of reproduction in whole or in part in any form. Published in the United States of America by Arbor House Publishing Company and in Canada by Fitzhenry & Whiteside, Ltd.

Parts of this book appeared, in different form, in *Geo, The Atlantic, Harper's, The New York Times Book Review, Audience, Playboy, The Berkeley Monthly, Cosmopolitan, Playgirl, Oui,* the *Los Angeles Times,* and *Travel & Leisure.* Gratitude to all of them, and to editors who indulged my curiosity and desire to walk. —H.G.

Library of Congress Catalog Card Number: 80-70216

ISBN: 0-87795-305-8 cloth edition

0-87795-322-8 Priam trade paperback edition

Manufactured in the United States of America

10 9 8 7 6 5 4 3 2 1

Contents

I. INTRODUCTION 7
   1. Some Misconnections of Soul in California 9

II. CALIFORNIA PLACES 23
   2. Presenting! The World's Greatest Post-Urban Process!:"Moonchild, You Will Pass Some Very Happy Romantic Moments in Los Angeles" 25
   3. San Francisco: The City That Asks if You Came 48
   4. How the Village of Palm Springs Became P*A*L*M S*P*R*I*N*G*S 68
   5. Whatever Happened to Big Sur? 81

III. LONELY ONES, MAKING OUT 95
   6. A Zen Hike with Bill Graham 98
   7. A Twenty-Year Talk with William Saroyan 109

IV.	LANGUAGE AND LINGO, ART AND STYLE	117
	8. Hunting the Wild Bromide	119
	9. Creatively Writing the Grippingly Erotic True Story	123
	10. Movies for Teevee—The Pride and the Money, The Sorrows and the Aggravation	132
V.	LIFE ON THE BRINK	149
	11. No Goddamn Body Stays Married Anymore	151
	12. Ballad of the Freeway Father	169
	13. "The Therapist Will See You Now, Big Boy" (Deep Carpet: The Tragic Bust of the Golden Gate Foundation)	180
	14. Their Karma Runs over His Dogma (A Sad Story of Sex in San Francisco)	197
	15. Maxifamily Doings in San Francisco	204
	16. Hi! Sex Is Not Located Only in the Head!	210
	17. Blind, Blind Date	216
	18. The Post-Hip Generation	227
	19. The Rise of the People People	231

I
INTRODUCTION

1
Some Misconnections of Soul in California

All California can be divided into as many parts as France, Texas, or any normal human place. "Eureka! I have found it!" has been the official motto of the state of California since the gold rush, but the secret motto is: *Yikes! I'm Looking for It.*

In this walk through California, a place on the brink of itself, at the extremest west side of America, I'd like to keep in the back of the mind certain matters while others come naturally to the front—that's what a stroll is about. Here are a few of the Californias that lie behind and even support the places, styles, and people I've spent these years looking at.

The ranching and farming inland valleys, where Slim and Pardner, Earl and Floyd, roam through both agribusiness and agrilegend. The morning mists are nice on the fields. But when the mists burn off at noon, you may find the children of Slim and Tex at play with their bikes and bombs in front of the Bank of America or the Pacific Gas and Electric power stations.

INTRODUCTION

The John Birch and Impeach Welfare Shirkers Orange and San Diego County, Disneyland, Navy, straight-arrow, love-it-or-leave-it slurbia, which has copious pockets wherever strong men and women gather to commute, even near San Francisco and San Jose.

The lumbering north, with conservationists clinging like bugs to the logs. "Seen one tree, want to see more." Some of the coastal towns used to do a lot of fishing and they're pretty quiet now. Want to start a commune? Folks can buy a motel, an urban mansion in Yreka, or a whole mining town, complete with nails from the True Boom, and some do. Marijuana is now the major crop in counties north of San Francisco. Anti-marijuana enforcement provides another source of income. Aerospace desolation row, where the Ph.D. engineers fight over hack licenses. Some find work busing the school kids hither and yon through barricades put up by Militant Mothers for Other Ideas. Professors and scientists are reduced to panning for gold in last century's mines. It's not glamorous to be a poorer country than we used to be.

A covert California, embarrassed amid the Nirvanas of est and fresh avocados, Hunger Project and marathon runs, is following the traditional path in reverse—*back* to Oklahoma, Ohio, Georgia, and even eccentric and dreaded Manhattan. There exists a California that doesn't work out even for misfits.

Those are not parallel categories for comparison, are they? That's California for you.

Anybody else, including you and me with a different brand of coffee coursing through our veins, could count many other Californias. The liberal, the conservative, the New-Left (with its antique ally, the Old-Left), the communal, the rockal, the countercultural now taken to the woods after the shipwrecks of the Sunset Strip and the Haight-Ashbury . . . Oh, listen, I even found an antique surfing-and-Hesse crew in La Jolla, near San Diego, gathered with their perfect tans and off-white hair in a head-and-bookshop complex allied to a 16mm, art movie house, a Safeway of the future, giving Blue Chip stamps with purchase of Paul Krassner's collected essays.

The spicy, morose Mexican-American ghettos. The black powder kegs in every major California city—just like in America. And the monster school population of universities, colleges, private and public, junior colleges, community colleges, extension branches, providing higher education for a number of students equal to the total population of some perfectly respectable members of the United Nations. Despite the foreclosures of funds, books are still cracked; many of the laboratories are still buying Bunsen burners if you promise to find a cure for cancer or what used to be called "juvenile delinquency" (now it's called "the kids"). On Hayakawa's diminished San Francisco State campus, for years there was no cafeteria place for gathering anymore past early afternoon (cafeterias lead straight to revolution) and hungry former strikers were reduced to morose brown-bagging in the winter rains. Of course, there were still those coffee and candy machines at the base of stairwells constructed by Sacramento engineers as their answer to Frank Lloyd Wright. And now there is a Student Union again—the danger is over.

Where are we meeting now? is my favorite California graffito.

The blue VW buses are going elsewhere.

The blue VW buses, vans, and campers seem to be going nowhere, parked at the curb, dropouts from city and country dropped into the heaven of mobility. Some are in school or not in school; some work or do not work; they are just waiting for something to happen. Dawn comes, and the civic folks in the ranch houses look out their windows to confront a rising tide of campers. It's Carnation Instant Breakfast versus yeast-and-tofu time, a morning gruel countdown in the new West. It takes awhile, for no one knows quite what to say. Americans are nice, Californians are nicest, and these must be someone's children parked at the curb to live in sin.

Across the generation gap come the imprecations of the eighties:

How can you afford *real estate?*

How can *you* afford gas?

COMPASSION IT UP A LITTLE, PLEASE

A distinguished American actor from the misty island of Manhattan wished to meet a distinguished American playwright in the far countree of Beverly Hills. The actor had appeared in the playwright's play at the American Place Theater; the movie would surely need him. Hearing that the playwright was starstruck, with the innocence of a boy—his style at forty-two was that of a wise but detached eleven-year-old—the actor got his number from Celebrity Service and telephoned.

"Please come right over," said the Playwright in a fragment of waste-free, fuel-injection, new-cinema dialogue.

The wise but detached forty-two-year-old eleven-year-old had uttered, and having uttered, hung up. The actor jumped into his Avis Impala and found his way through canyon and across firebreak to curving driveway leading to Greek Revival Golden West Savings & Loan Mainstream Redwood Academy Award Ranch House. Playwright's wife rested upstairs, recovering from hysterectomy and reading *Variety.* Playwright himself greeted handsome, jut-jawed—and here real life brings us a remarkable fictional touch—*intelligent,* distinguished American actor. Host ushered guest to a comfortable cast-iron chair by a cozy pool, all the while chatting of early Ford grant, middle Community Theater hits, late bonanza in low-budget sleeper drawn from prosification of

Some Misconnections of Soul in California 13

verse tragedy first offered as a Hopwood Prize Play at the University of Michigan.

Actor, with the shrewdness unusual to his kind, noticed that Playwright was nervous about meeting *him.* Actor relaxed. Playwright paced, offered refreshment, made joke about the President, volunteered recent gossip about the Industry, expressed nostalgia for the independence of a poet or novelist, named daughter away at boarding school, asked if Actor would like to see writing cottage in garden, award citations, letter files, scrapbook.

The telephone rang. Actor overheard the following conversation while tossing cork coasters into pool and watching them float away amid widening chlorine ripples which symbolize, here, a choked anxiety and sinus condition. "What? Oh, hi Carlene. What? He did? *What?* But I just saw him on the tennis court this morning. He looked wonderful—slim. Tanned. Are you sure? That's terrible. Oh, I'm sorry, Carlene . . . Gee, I'd like to come over, but I have a friend here now, we're having a meeting, maybe if you're sure, you should just call the police—"

He looked puzzled at the phone. The party at the other end had hung up.

A clatter of slippers down the outer stairway. It was Playwright's wife, who had heard enough of the conversation and was on her way next door, where a neighbor had just dropped dead. Playwright watched his wife sprinting past the pool, heedless of her recent surgery, and gradually it came to him that some explanation was in order. He cleared his throat.

"It's not as if we were close friends," he said. "He does realistic drama, teevee scripts, Odets, Robert Anderson, Paddy, that sort of thing—I'm into black humor with more of a poetic touch, you know, lots of spaces between the words—Pinter, Beckett, Albee . . . pauses. . . ."

Actor was getting up to leave.

"I don't get much chance," said Playwright, "out here in lotusland, to talk with a real representative of the serious American theater like you . . ."

He was following the actor to his Avis Impala. Actor was unable to think of words to put pauses between. He slipped into driving position, a big man but intelligent. He said good-bye.

Playwright burst out: "Shit, man, he just happened to live next door!"

JOSE FERRER, DID YOU EVER GET YOUR MAIL?

The Cory Gallery in San Francisco is one of those all-ya-can art supermarkets. The Eyes of Walter Keane were upon it, but Walter Keane has slipped into astigmatic eclipse as the tourists, tired of Fisherman's Wharf and cable car rides, seek a souvenir of even more Lasting Value than that hyperthyroid grief. Cory follows the honorable habit of guaranteeing his stable of fast-painting stylists a living wage in return for regular doses of French Impressionism, Hudson River American, Dufy Boats & Skies, Chagallesque rabbis, cows, and violinists, abstracts dripped by Tinguely painting machines, anything that can be done reasonably quickly. As a sales lure, for years he had a subtle touch: the package wrapped for mailing (no postage affixed) and left in a conspicuous corner of the gallery. The name on the sticker, writ large in India ink, was "Jose Ferrer, Hollywood, California." Ferrer played Toulouse-Lautrec, you may recall, and came to painting in this stumpy phase. I also seem to recall dusty packages addressed to Vincent Price.

The star of the Cory Pantheon was Pat Cucaro, the future

old master, said to be on a retainer of $50,000 a year, which meant producing a painting almost every hour during a forty-hour week. Publicity for the Cory Gallery exploited the syllogism; Picassos once sold cheaply, now those who bought them are rich. Cucaros are now relatively inexpensive; therefore those who buy today will have a thing of beauty and a powerful hedge against inflation.

Mr. Cory himself seemed genuinely fond of painting, and often gave away his work to friends and customers as souvenirs of the operation.

36,000 BOOKS PUBLISHED THIS YEAR, NOT COUNTING *ANNA KARENINA*

Beverly Hills long ago supplanted Manhattan as the all-purpose favorite No Soul Country of myth and dream. Of course, that's a variety of genocide; everyone on this earth has feelings, privacy, desire for intimacy and community, mortal dreads, birth visions, love fantasies, truth ambitions.

But some places put special burdens on the deepest human intentions. California is one such place. Southern California is another. Zen contemplation, consciousness-raising, communal force-feeding of hearts, touch encounters, franchised sorcerer's apprentices, est and lifespring and Arica, nude beaches, sixteen-track stereo are all worthy efforts to get in touch with depth.

Sometimes the depth-seeking seems merely a subdivision of the problem of knowledge and intelligence. A professor at UCLA delivers a lecture on *Anna Karenina,* and a tall, handsome, blond lad with surf-dried skin and the dropout mustache—suave, countrified, hip—comes up after class and comments, "I like that book, especially because it's about

Russians. We got to know all we can about the Russians. My dad made that clear to me when I was a kid. This boy write other good things?"

It turned out, under closer questioning, that the young Slavophile had read *War and Peace, Resurrection,* and maybe *Hadji Murad* and *What Is Art?* during his Evelyn Wood Reading Dynamics phase. But the only book by Tolstoy he really remembered was *Crime and Punishment,* because he saw a revival of the flick with Yul Brynner.

This young man, you say, can be found all over the land?

But not so handsome, serious, blond, and honest. And not so likely to be a speed-reader.

AND NOW SOME PSYCHOLOGY TO GO WITH THE AFORESAID SOCIAL PHILOSOPHY

The Flavor of the Month at Baskin-Robbins is Identity Crisis Blah. California itself, like the character of the graduate student bank robber in a San Francisco novel of the sixties, *The Great American Jackpot,* is Not Guilty by Reason of Jumpiness.

Those students who slip into their backpacks in the morning as their older brothers and sisters (now Mr. and Ms.) put on their Peace buttons are looking for Arcadia within the Dream of Arcadia. If they find only hepatitis, it's not for lack of poignant search, guided by the honest primitive instincts of Herman Hesse and Baba Ram Dass.

Meanwhile, in the cities, the penitential agonies of the liberals continue. A book by Peter Drucker has revealed his analysis of current demographic studies: *Americans aren't as young as they were only a few years ago.* The same thing is true of the current-events activist freaks who throw themselves into every yearly Third-World fad (remember Frantz

Fanon? Eldridge Cleaver? fish-ins for the Indians, starring Mr. Brando and Ms. J. Fonda?). A middle-aged Jewish writer with a Sephardic name recently insisted on reading in an Evening of Third World Poetry at Occidental College. Getting radicalized to the left or right makes for cottage industry in California.

ETERNAL VALUE

The history of Judaism contains a fair share of miracles and marvels, though not so many, of course, as in Christianity, which specialized. Here is one true vision of California Judaism respectfully submitted for the annals of modern piety. Away down in Orange County, far from Jerusalem or Kamenets-Podolskiy, in the aerospace slurb which stretches through the ghosts of fruit groves from the L.A. basin toward the Mexican border, there stands a lonely, dusty, stucco synagogue, surrounded by fading billboards pleading for the repeal of income tax and the release of hostages in Iran. This is not the dopey California; this is straight-arrow and right wing. If there are speed freaks in town, they are only the twice-born kids of once-born parents, supplementing a diet of pizza and frozen yogurt with a little Methedrine crystal for the nerves.

These people may be different, but they are still people. Their conventions about food stamps, blacks, Southeast Asia, cities, country, and fresh air may be different from yours and mine. But soothed by the times and irritated by history, they are human beings.

A small group of Jews lives among them in the bent pocket between two cloverleafs and an Interstate.

This lost fragment invited me to come to speak to them of Things Jewish, Things Novelistic, Things In General. The man who picked me up at a feeder airport had only one arm —war hero. He drove a special car and also, he informed me, flew his own plane. He was a temporarily unemployed aeronautics engineer. He was also, as he said... "the Deacon of the Synagogue."

We drove and drove through the gathering winter dark. Yes, there is a sort of winter in Southern California—grayness, damp chill, early nightfall. It was more than fifty miles to the synagogue. After my talk, there were drinks and food, bagels, cream cheese, corned beef, mint patties, and then he loaded me into his special car and drove me fifty miles to catch a midnight flight home to San Francisco. Round trip for him would be over two hundred miles this evening. He said he does it for all the synagogue speakers.

"Why?"

"Oh, I like to meet celebrities from the outside world. For example, two months ago we had a Hassidic rabbi from New York, and last month we had the chief test pilot from Lockheed, and now—you."

Said the one-armed Jewish deacon from Orange County as we cruised the freeway at a precise highway-patrol-safe speed of just ten miles above the limit: "I get to talk privately with the individual. I get to exchange ideas and feelings. I'll drive or fly a million miles, sir, if only I can get in touch with some serious persons of the Jewish persuasion."

THE ETERNAL RETURN

This girl. This lovely thing who carried the Twist from the Rhythm Room of the Airport Holiday Inn straight into my heart. She was once a Majorette Champion of Orange and Lockheed Tri-Star Queen of Burbank, then rode her frisky I.Q. to Stanford, complained that her parents had money for a swimming pool but none for art, culture, and skiing, wrote poetry which she submitted to the *New Yorker,* printed a book review in the *Berkeley Barb* (proposed publication of her Collected Review), enlisted in the legions of flower children in San Francisco, departed after several simultaneous unhappy love affairs with men who all did her wrong during the same busy summer. She joined Swinging London in the role of that item as exotic and delicious in Europe as the Duck-Billed Platypus—*a California girl,* and finally came home to marry a young doctor who had never given up his pursuit of her. She still works out with her baton. They are living happily ever afterward in Encino (condominium, football weekends, and a swimming pool which her daughter may someday condemn as she condemned her own parents').

In a few years her daughter will pass through the majorette and SALT-3 Missile Queen phase. And listen with grotesque sighs of boredom while her mum tells how Sno-Cones, Softies, and Acapulco Gold used to taste better in the old days. What she'll do about it is still a mystery. A story, even that familiar one about fate—Vico, Plato, and the eternal return—should always end in mystery; California is less a country of the mind than one of the playful imagination —a story which ends with another story.

ENVOI AND WHAT WORDS PROVE

George Jackson is still dead. Eldridge Cleaver is born again, this time for the first time into his new religion, Chrislam, which takes a little from Christianity and a little from Islam, and also preaches wife-beating as a form of discipline and trousers with codpieces as a form of, well, letting it all hang out. Grass is not yet legal, despite predictions by the various soothsayers to the unknown of the past two decades. Tim Leary and the Black Panthers are yesterday's game, sometimes brought out for the Sunday paper like your old frisbee or psychedelic black-light poster. (And where are the Diggers now? Emmett Grogan, that charming hustler, used to telephone me with news of his books and died of an overdose on a New York subway train.)

The rumble outside my door is the sound of Californies packing up their station wagons, heading east on the Interstate, back to Oklahoma. When it's dust versus smog, that old dust tastes just fine.

The Beach Boys are alive. You can almost say as much for Troy Donahue.

The surf is still up.

Aerospace experts in the southland, L.A. and Orange, are boning up on mass transit, trains, subways, hydrofoils, as they drive those Yellow Cabs just for a little spending money. San Francisco is bringing ferries back to the Bay and still promising to tear down freeways. Some smart boys bought vineyards for use in the actual growing of wine grapes; some won, some lost. When the first housing development is leveled to convert the land to viticulture, a decisive step will be taken, turning history backwards in this last outpost and glory of American optimism. Time and mortality, friends, have gained on the West Coast.

California still dreaming.

My eureka problem and yours.

WHAT WORDS PROVE

Words prove nothing. Need we draw conclusions about California from the aforesaid gleanings of evidence? All things are related, the Buddhists and other thinkers tell us;

and therefore, if we are using the language correctly, if we are using head and soul correctly, if we are using heart and mind, experience and history, hope and dream, intention and doubt, all things are also unrelated.

The anticommunards living by the side of the road in their VW buses, the wise but detached eleven-year-old playwright, the Tolstoy-loving surfer, the sweet weaver's old lady, who doesn't want to be a sexist's slave anymore, as blacks and students are, Senator S. I. ("Don") Hayakawa, the one-armed Orange County synagogue deacon, my dear friend the platypus, they are all bemused and lonely, they are the just plain folks of California. I haven't mentioned the potato farmers of Shafter, the longshoremen of Stockton, the masses in the ghettos and the masses trying to keep them there. I haven't mentioned the struggles against elitism, agism, weightism (a University of California scholar recently published a book in defense of hefties). I haven't mentioned drugs, except for a little speed, or war and the draft, unless you count the aerospace industry a part of the military economy. I've only hinted here about the cycle of inflation and depression.

California is special, typical, hopeless, and still full of hope. It's a part of the main. When the beatniks metamorphosed into the hippies, and the postwar boom segued into the Viet Nam wartime boom, and "California Dreamin'" became a national anthem, there occurred one of those rare moments when an entire nation tried to live out a partial myth. It came to San Francisco to wear flowers in its hair. The flowers wilted. People left their hearts in San Francisco, and the maids took them to the hotel lost and found departments. Although there are still slices of Berkeley in almost every college town, and little Sunset Strips or Haight-Ashburys in every big city, minigrokkers and groovers everywhere, California in the eighties has floated partway back toward the general American reality. Which doesn't mean that the myth has washed away. California still makes out the weird best way it can, and when that doesn't work, as often it doesn't, it is still ready to try another way *immediately.* This anonymous friskiness is part of both the optimism and despair of California. It depends on so much freedom, youth, availability of resource, even money, and none of these things seem to be permanent anymore.

The extreme isolation of life in California means that we travel, in a way reminiscent of the contemporary fate everywhere, on nerve. This can work out okay as long as the support systems remain in order—youth and health, work, love or some variation of it, little continuous pleasures and distractions. Family helps; things help. Weakness and failure definitely do not help. The spectacle of souls desperately cannibalizing themselves through drugs, cults, or the simple descent from sanity is a familiar one. Youth is not merely a fad out here; it often seems a requirement for the course. And since it is also a disease which time inevitably cures, there is a tragic outer edge to a career in California. Age, sleep, and death are inevitable, no matter how alertly famished the soul feels just now.

We don't really need space exploration. We have it right here.

II
CALIFORNIA PLACES

2
Presenting! The World's Greatest Post-Urban Process!: "Moonchild, You Will Pass Some Very Happy Romantic Moments in Los Angeles"

Once upon a time there was desert. Nearby there were also so many flowers you could walk noplace without stepping on blossoms. Then there were Indians, Spaniards, ranches and haciendas. And now there are highways, hideouts, dugouts, restaurants built like Indian temples and churches built like Chicago banks, money and poverty, aerospace and movies, airmen and *luftmenschen,* monuments on roller skates, culture, instant hope and ominous despair, and an atmosphere so green and thick at times you might want to write a message on it: HELP!

It was not supposed to be this way. The way it was supposed to be—sun and space, water and sea, *freedom*—also still exists. Mobility is the theme of Los Angeles, not stasis, monuments, concern for the past (*which* past?). It is called a city; it is, in fact, an immense post-urban process, the tentative validation of a concept New York only hints at and

Cleveland or Des Moines doesn't dare to express. But L.A. is settled by refugees from New York, Cleveland, and Des Moines, from the dust bowl and the South, from Heartland America. They are here for this. It is the first American experimental space colony on earth.

In Tahiti I picked up a leaflet from the L.A. tourist bureau which announced, in French, "Visitez l'Excitante Region de Los Angeles." It was a leaflet showing beaches, grass huts, tropical opulence almost identical with the touristic delights of the Society Islands. And yet it must be stated clearly, without any ambiguity, that Los Angeles is not Papeete.

In Los Angeles, just as the architecture sometimes seems a joke on history or nature—hamburger stand shaped like a toadstool, family dwelling like Hansel's and Gretel's house—so people sometimes grow into shapes different from what they must be elsewhere: transsexuals on Sunset Boulevard, being other genders; old men with young hair transplants, tucked facelifts, tennis-trained bodies; geriatric women with girls' intentions; and among the poor who fill all the freeway interstices, a less-known phenomenon—a youth which is withered and weary and dry of skin, like old folks elsewhere. Nathanael West described "bridges which bridged nothing, sculpture in trees, palaces that seemed of marble until a whole stone portico began to flap in the breeze." A generation later, this unsolid process has grown by a million or two, but it still flaps in the breeze.

If one is in Los Angeles rather than of Los Angeles, visiting rather than living, there can be a dizzying sense of lack of grasp of the place. But it turns out that native Angelenos suffer the same vertigo. They substitute for a city culture the community of sex, drugs, teevee or radio noise, sensation—that's the stereotype—and also the ones of community, of a neighborhood, of job, of family. The immense racketing city alters all these elements of shared humanity and produces feelings which are unlike those of earthlings elsewhere. No wonder Unidentified Flying Objects and men from space are sighted and credited so loyally in L.A. A bit of strange is quite to be expected. An otherwise tender love affair can break up because: "We got along fine. He was terrific. But he moved to another part of L.A."

Los Angeles doesn't tell the truth about itself or the world; it makes it up. It is like a hermetic work of art, a sculpture with reference to a purpose not meant for understanding. What seems to be sprawl and whim is really . . . whim and sprawl. But this random process comes because of intention and the will of men and women who wish to define themselves anew, see anew, make a new and energetic life for themselves on the old earth. Successive waves of westerners fell off the gold rush or trade with Australia; then came the ranchers, then oilers and railroaders, then invalids searching for health in the clean dry air of California, then business-hungry New Yorkers, then Okies from the dust bowl (L.A. police used to try to stop them at the borders), then aerospace and shipyard workers, blacks from the South and Orientals from the Orient, university people for the thinkeries, bureaucrats and sheriffs and even European adventurers . . . I met an English marrying duke in Westwood (his business was to marry widows, and he married one in my own family), who turned out to be a con man from Phoenix—he and his wife, my cousin, spent their days pasting up paper models of the furniture they had ordered and filled the house with flammable schemes . . . Starlets in diners. Hookers. Scavengers. Buddhists and guru-hunters and gurus. A baba from India who held my hand, saying, "You have a beautiful soul, a beautiful soul, I can tell what you are thinking." What I was thinking: how to get my hand out of his damp one? how to get out of this here Indian movie producer's six-hundred-thousand-dollar ashram? doesn't he have a serious head cold? (With his free hand he kept blowing his nose in a stack of orange washcloths.)

The movie producer's ashram was full of Texans, New Yorkers, divorcées, seekers. The orange groves and vineyards have receded, the cattle ranches have been tracted over, but the galloping seekers are still ripening on the vines.

Outside, a crazed loiterer was singing the classic song from *Shaft*. *Who is that black private dick, sex machine to all the chicks? Shaft. Damn right.* He was not a loiterer, he had a white coat on, like a doctor; he was the car-parker. He was parking the cars and serenading the guru-hungry and expecting a nice little tip. Damn right.

A generation ago, a Los Angeles guidebook whispered in your ear: "The world's most extensive system of interurban electric railway makes it easy to review the charms of this varied region, only an hour from the Sierra Madre to the sea, spinning through orange groves one minute, climbing a canyon pass the next . . . ."

No more, brother or sister. It is now off-ramp city, a gigantic feeder for airports and highways systems, with little blue punctuation marks of swimming pools, like freeform amoeba, seen from the air. Los Angeles has not been rural for awhile, but it is only recently trying to become a city. It is an enormous experiment in urban technology, heaving waste products into history. Oil derricks are pumping and automobiles are emitting. How easy to complain at the loss of the warm, cozy, muscular West. But as the human nerve is exposed like the scarring of freeways and canyons, Los Angeles has also become more, well, *interesting*. Oil pumps, like gigantic praying mantises, bob and bow in the *terrains vagues* along the freeways. This insect honeycomb, buzzing and burring, is the wildest side of America.

At a "Health Club" in Hollywood last year, forty men

were arrested for participating in a "slave auction," the slaves being young men offered for sale "for sexual purposes." A heck of a lot of handcuffs, chains, manacles, clamps, wooden stocks, and leather masks were confiscated. The "slaves" were either nude or accoutered in these odd garbs. The defense? It was "all in fun"; four of the participants later pled guilty to misdemeanor prostitution charges.

Sexual liberty and experimentation which seem "all in fun" in other parts of America somehow become the required course in this extreme corner. It is as if the disorganization of the city—the urban agglomeration, as it is often called—makes for an exaggeration of personal whim and fantasy. With little support from neighborhood and tradition, the metaphysical extremes of love as eroticism must do all the work of defining and affirming personality. In solitude comes the lonely scream: the scream of automobile tires on the freeway, of the imaginary victims in the hundreds of detective novels set in L.A., of the slaves and masters at their grim charades of violence and love. Next door there is the cackle of the Indian baba or the Born-Again bondage merchant.

Or, since this is also a city of families, the pleased racket of the kids on skateboards, flying daringly up and down the slopes of a construction site. The children are filled with health, energy, fun, and pilot's glee. It often seems as if all the entertaining madness is only a subtext for the normal persistence of a tough citizenry camped out amid this immense, permanent construction site.

No other great city locates a black, bubbling, surly stench as a major tourist attraction. Los Angeles presents the La Brea Tar Pits, the world's largest ice age fossil deposit embedded in a lake of asphalt. The Indians used the tar to caulk their canoes; the white man used it for roofing. Now we visitors stand on a concrete observation platform. Below, there is water of a suspicious color, and slow giant bubbles rhythmically explode at the surface, as if the ancient mammoths and tigers and camels are still breathing within eons of accretion of tar. For thirty thousand years animals stepped into this lake to drink; they were caught in the ooze; they howled and shrieked; tigers leaped onto their backs to eat. They ate, and then the tigers also followed the slimy bones into the pits. Wolves, vultures, camels, mastodons, monsters which no longer haunt the earth, birds which no longer fly the skies sank into this mess. Some escaped by clinging to overhanging trees. Millions died. Saber-toothed cats with knifelike fangs, an extinct eagle larger than the condor, elephants, bisons, bears, multitudes of roaring and howling and squawling creatures sank and turned and, in murk and slow turmoil forevermore, were preserved.

The George C. Page Museum of La Brea Discoveries opened a few years ago. It is constructed like an earthen burial mound to evoke the dwelling of the hundreds of tons of fossils recovered from the tar. One sinks into the museum, children slipping and sliding down the roof and walls, almost as the animals once slid into the pits (the children laugh and howl, however, they do not perish, snarling). Exhibits show tiger bones turning back into tiger, woman bones turning into woman. The skeletons were petrified in tar—boars, flamingos, lions, condors, and that single lorn nine-thousand-year-old lady. ("How was it to die there?" I asked her soul. "Lonely," she replied.)

The La Brea Tar Pits used merely to exist there on Wilshire Boulevard in Hancock Park for millions of years before Wilshire Boulevard and Hancock Park existed. The smell was bad. History often does smell strong and rancid. Angelenos joked about it, but only recently came the vision of the Tar Pits as History—as a monument to what lived on these busy streets before Man, and what still lives, shifting and bubbling, below these busy streets. Museum visitors can watch the white-coated scientists patching the fossils together. "This will be a mastodon. This will be a dire wolf. This is an extinct bird's toenail, preserved in ooze."

This is not Disneyland, honey.

Natural gas can be mined here. The museum building floats on a sea of oil, and will only tip like a rowboat in an earthquake (they hope), and then tip back.

On Sundays, when the tourists come, you can sometimes buy belt buckles and jewelry and stained-glass frogs in the park. Flower children recovered like fossils from the Summer of Love are selling homemade chocolate chip cookies. And if you dig in the soil beneath the new grass, and if you're lucky or unlucky, an ooze of tar swells beneath your fingernails. This is not astro-silt. This is genuine bowel ooze from the earth's great ecosystem.

If California is a country of the mind, as Kevin Starr has written, San Francisco may be its ego and Los Angeles its id. Stretching Freud's categories a little too much, we might include in the special id of Los Angeles a lot of libido and double-knit stretch pants. San Francisco, exploding with the gold rush of 1849, exploded by earthquake and fire a half century later, reexploding enthusiastically into new growth, defined the early image of California for the rest of the world. But in this century, the discovery of oil, the film industry, new kinds of manufacturing, the railways, ports, and highways, all contributed to Los Angeles's brashly taking charge of California. Millions of people came to the south of the state, searching for clean air and fortunes. (Sometimes they found the latter; they lost the former.) The division of power in California took on a classic American Civil War shape: San Francisco pretty and settled and prematurely ripe; Los Angeles brash and ugly and rich and poor and filled with interstices into which a person could slip to dreamland or ruin. "You may be too much for Memphis, Baby," a popular song wailed, "but you're not enough for L.A."

L.A. is no longer what it used to be: orange and walnut country, a great plain sloping to the sea, an average temperature of sixty-two clean degrees. In 1830 there were about seven hundred residents, in 1890 the population was fifty thousand. From 1900 to 1950, Los Angeles doubled its population every decade. Now, within nearly five hundred square miles—surely the most extended city in the world—there are millions of souls and about as many orange groves as there are vineyards in Paris. As the air has degenerated and the plain was covered with slurb, sprawl, and highway, so the optimism of the city of angels has turned rusty at the edges. A "small boom" used to be mourned like a depression. Now, after aerospace became a great industry and then fell victim to the rearrangement of priorities—one of my cab drivers was a laid-off aerospace engineer—optimistic hustle is laminated throughout the noncommunity with cynicism, with find-yourself groupiness, with laid-back abandon, with ghetto and minority resentments, with a degree of rage and self-doubt. San Diego and San Jose have muscled against L.A., much as Los Angeles muscled San Francisco down. In a way, the Hispanic pueblo has reclaimed its own. Communication is not by covered wagon and ship, and in business Los Angeles sometimes seems to be a branch office of New York—witness the financing and control of the film industry—but it is still a little romantic national consciousness of its own. Perhaps it should claim individual membership in the United Nations. Los Angeles is as weird, special, and as hungry for development as many member nations.

Sometimes Los Angeles is portrayed as a foolish and irrational early-computer readout of highways and sprawl, the sagebrush skittering across asphalt and concrete, the people doing the same. This is mostly wrong, or at least partially so. Los Angeles was the first major breakthrough of Motorized Man into what might be called Hallucinatory Reality—the fantasy of sweet air and total pleasure, houses that are castles and theaters which are palaces, cathedrals, or mosques. No matter that the lungers who fled to Los Angeles for the sweet air eventually found "atmospheric inversion" (smog). No matter that the canyon houses slide into mud and the movie cathedrals became the bankrupt victims of television. The vision remains. David Soul, once The Covered Man—a rock singer in a paper bag—came out of his paper bag to try to be an idolized blond television star; and he wonders in the *Gay Advocate,* a homosexual newspaper, if . . . "if I'm a full-blown artist yet."

Intelligence and fantasy are employed everywhere. Visitors and those formed by tradition, any tradition, may not recognize the artifacts as the products of higher functions in human nature. But it took an energetic mind to imagine and construct the clock of the Hollywood Ranch Market, spinning wildly backwards and forwards, randomly furious, to indicate that whatever time you think it is, it's always time, night and day, to shop at the Hollywood Ranch Market. This is hallucinatory reality because The Covered Man and the Hollywood Ranch Market are not the dreams of madness and failure, mere smoke in the head—they are realized, they exist and prosper, those enchanted forests and Trianon cottages and Hansel-and-Gretel sugar mansions.

And of course they also attract failure from all over. There is the mad killer of blacks and the mad killer of whites, a Jack the Ripper for hookers and one for homosexuals. There are Viet Nam sharpshooters who fire at motorists from freeway overpasses; there are arsonists and druggies. Failure can be astounding. It is even possible to invent a new psychiatry, a new form of group therapy, and not make a go of it. The most unimaginable enterprises can also sink out of sight in the tar pits.

But the photochemicals of L.A. are different, and failure is tinted bizarrely. The old folks of Venice, its canals silted over, the nostalgic real estate crumbling into condo development, can sit by the sea to watch an endless tape loop of human need, loss, hope, beach joggers, plus a few muggings. Marina del Mar, next door, takes care of the younger swingers. Someone has said that the air is often so chemical-laden that you don't need developer for your photographs; just hang them out on a line.

What one calls hallucinatory reality could be called the Mad Too Much in Watts, the black ghetto, in East L.A., the brown ghetto, and in the San Fernando Valley, the immense sprawling lower-middle-class white-bread ghetto. Of course, there are blacks, browns, and whites nearly everywhere; the boundaries are not neat; the entire city, seen from Mars, is an integrated ghetto. The daughters of San Fernando Valley run away to Tijuana with the guitarists from East L.A. who can't read music, with the drummers from Watts who are sort of looking for a good punk rock gig that doesn't interfere with just hanging out on the Sunset Strip. The Watts Towers, glued together over a lifetime by an obsessed Italian artisan, has become the cultural monument of Watts, although it reminds everyone of Italy and not of the black Americans who live there. Elsewhere, illegal Mexican immigrants chow up in Tacorias built of formica, glass, and astroturf on Angeleno versions of Tex-Mex border food, sold to them by franchise conglomerates headquartered in New York banks. In the San Fernando Valley, swing clubs of wife-swappers discuss the aerospace business or the problems of power lawn mowers before my wife gently leads your husband into the Play Room. (The rules: you must not criticize anyone's real spouse, you must not issue a critique of sexual performance, you must be friendly, kind, reserved, though erotically inventive and scrubbed in body.)

This may seem unbelievable. It is firmly rooted in midair.

It's easy to fall, describing Los Angeles, into nightmare language, as if the dislocation of our sense of city and country, place and domain, requires hallucination. And yet there is also a cozy daymare quality about the hundreds of neighborhoods which make up this enormous city-state. With inventive persistence, gays have found their places, movie people, engineers, geriatrics, immigrants from the South, blacks, Hispanics, failures, successes. Of course, these are not exclusive and parallel categories, and in an odd way the city, uncontrolled in its lurch and sprawl, reminds me of a favorite daymare city of mine, Port-au-Prince, Haiti. The categories are all mixed. In Beverly Hills, where it used to be (once happened to me) that the police stopped people for *walking* —"what are you doing here? let me see your identification" —there are also now the young and poor and vaguely laid back. There are joggers. Not every stroller is automatically assumed to be a rapist or a burglar. The police have longer hair and tempers are mellowing with the emotional gains of the sixties. Los Angeles now has an earnest, soft-spoken black mayor. While the flower child colony of the Sunset Strip was pruned by drugs and riots, police and porn, kid excesses and adult overreaction, something of a San Francisco strolling street-theater ease persists there, and also on Hollywood Boulevard, and in Silverlake and Westwood, and near UCLA and the other campuses which dot this city which has more colleges and universities than most nations. A barren stretch of road, with nothing but gas pumps and franchise feeding troughs, is suddenly interrupted by a *soukh*—markets, stalls, coffee houses, bars, live people on legs, putting one shoe ahead of the next—*walking.*

That there are large black, Japanese, Chicano, Chinese, and Russian communities which guard their ethnic purity is well known. There are also extended families of those faithful to UFOs and Scientology, and you can listen to soft Scientological rock on an L. Ron Hubbard radio station. There are those who converse in tongues and those awaiting a call from mail-order prophets who bless cripples and change the tires on their wheelchairs. The Mexicans live uneasily beside the blacks and the transplanted southerners and dustbowl refugees who have, in general and relatively, prospered. East Los Angeles College, where I once lectured, has a mainly black and brown student body. A professor of English, who had spent a previous career as an Army officer stationed in Germany, informed me: "This is not one of those fancy classic educations we give here. We teach them to fill out forms and put the commas inside the quotation marks and how to write the possessives. I want my students to make good cops, soldiers, and clerks. I want them to know how to use credit cards. They're good kids, and if I kick ass a little, they learn."

No, East Los Angeles College is not Harvard or Stanford, but when I spoke to these students about American literature, they wanted to know: Who are the great black writers and why? Who are the great brown writers and why? Where is the epic novel about how the Chinese worked the railroads that made this town prosper? Sir, have you read *Longtime Californ*, that anthology of Asian writing about California?

In the census of 1970, Los Angeles and New York showed great similarities as the commanding metropolises of the Pacific and Atlantic coasts. As ports and commercial centers they were comparable, and they came out about the same for population stability, educational levels, crime levels, numbers of doctors and dentists (more faith healers in L.A., more voodoo doctors in N.Y.), average family income (about $11,000 per year in 1970, before the recent inflation). The great difference was population growth and exchange. New Yorkers move to California, rarely the reverse. And nearly forty-five thousand people from New York City had moved to Los Angeles during the previous decade.

They were not going for the clean air or the tacos. They were not going for money, since Los Angeles is not richer than New York. They were going because it is still El Dorado, the golden promised land, to which Americans pay soul service. And the blue VW vans of the kids, and the piled-high Avis rent-a-trucks of the young families, still continued the trek westward during the slowed-down, less-prosperous, less-mobile seventies.

Near the campus of Short Hills Community College a middle-aged man in the uniform of a professor of the fifties, tweed jacket, pipe, neatly trimmed pepper-and-salt mustache (regimental in England, professorial here), was walking along the street at dusk with a toddler. He was smiling. The child could have been his grandson or his son by a second or third marriage. He was puffing his pipe and smiling and sharply cracking the child on the rear and legs while the child screamed and begged him to stop and alternately ran away (man caught up with him and gave him a harder swat) or clung to his legs, crying, "Please don't don't don't I promise," and there was a clawing jerk out of this embrace from below which seemed to enrage the smiling man and another hard crack. Before my eyes—cling and beg? run away?—I could see the child receiving an adult lesson in hopelessness. He had no chance.

I crossed the street and ran toward the two. I was a stranger in town. They belonged. The man looked up at me quizzically, took the pipe out of his mouth, and said in soft easy tones, "He has to learn not to run into the street. He crosses the curb before I tell him to."

The boy was hiccuping and sobbing at this respite, and staring at me. The only thing I could think to do was to stand there and watch. Still sobbing, the child toddled along beside his guardian. The man puffed his pipe and did not hit him. They turned the corner, and as they disappeared from sight, I heard a piercing shriek.

On that quiet suburban street there was chaos. There had always been chaos on that street, but now the man and his child made it visible. They had together even brought a bit of excitement into this clean, calm world—the child's hysteria, the man's sadism and pleasure made sweeter by his sense that it was a necessary discipline, the communication of energy which flooded me like sexual bliss. And since none of this could have a happy outcome, it was chaos.

In Westwood, near the University of California campus, even the beggars are stylish. A bum looked at my beard and jeans and said, "Are you one of them or one of us?" And another asked me not for whiskey or coffee, but: "Hey, Mister, gimme a quarter for a frozen yogurt."

Angelenos often have a large provincial sophistication about the rest of the world. They think big and they think possessively. In a real estate office in Westwood, the boom in property values makes the air vibrate with bizarre prosperity. Inner cities die, the barrio explodes with music from radios on windowsills, ghettoes burn, but Malibu, Westwood, Marina del Mar, Santa Monica inflate. A salesman who has earned "too much" this year—taxes—told me, "I gotta go to Europe in October. I've never seen that part of the country."

If you slide onto a Los Angeles freeway and drive and drive and drive, and then pull off the freeway, you might find something different from what you left. Or you might find another stretch of neighborhood, many canyons and hills and plains away, which is just like the one you left—palm trees, palmy breezes, swimming pools, gray photosynthetic air. It is written in a holy text: "Paradise is only for those who have already been there." To escape L.A., you may have to go there.

I remember when the dust bowl farmers of the thirties fled to California, their belongings heaped on their Fords, their faces drawn and embittered. Many of them grew rich on ranches which later became urban L.A. The grapes of wrath were stamped into wine.

I remember when the aging of Cleveland and Detroit and Chicago and New York decided, after the war, to strike out anew for the all-year garden cuddliness of Los Angeles. It was before the word *smog* had come into the vocabulary. Some of them died of emphysema; now, if they made their fortunes and have grown old, they have fled to Palm Springs, where little tendrils of smog follow them.

The air. How can we talk about Los Angeles, that basin of thermal anarchy, without the Smog? It provides a moral haze while it breaks down the lung tissue. The rich try to escape it by moving to Malibu or Santa Monica, or by climbing the hills; but smears and wisps follow silently after them, like werewolves, like Dracula, like the sins of Man, sucking at their lives. Shoeleather erodes. Eyes smart. School children are told on certain days not to play. The freeways snake throughout this world larger than many nations and the motors emit, emit, emit. Photosynthesis. Ozone. Inversion. The radio weather helicopters hover over the stalled rush-hour traffic and, between Scientology rock music and sweet whispers of laid-back true love, tell the world: "Air quality today not so good . . . turn off your engines if you can . . ." And the commuters are late because of an accident, jamming the freeway. Francis Gary Powers, once the U-2 pilot shot down over the USSR, the one who didn't use his CIA cyanide needle, who caused Ike to squirm and Khrushchev to bellow, died in the crash of a weather helicopter. Someone had forgotten to fill the gas tanks.

Sing a Song of L.A. air, that product which sometimes makes one want to be a minnow or a shark, living in a friendlier salt element. No wonder people smoke, drink, brag, and switch wives. And yet there are gardens growing, space in the alleys for flowers, poolside loungers—pools everywhere—old people, on Social Security, and young folks, starting out in life as post office clerks, who live in apartment complexes constructed around the pool.

When San Francisco was in a water panic due to drought, and angry with L.A. for the canals which divert its water southwards, and rationing water, friends from the Southland were telephoning long distance and playing the sounds of flushing toilets and giggling madly.

Society West, an attempt to authenticate for Los Angeles and its satellites the idea of an aristocracy, is a magazine filled with horse shows, news of formal dances for children, and flashes like: "Mort Ballagh sold his house in Trousdale and has taken an apartment in one of those high rises on the beach. It's a lot chummier . . . Speaking of moving, I understand that Jack Hupp, realtor, has just sold a house in Trousdale to a Saudi Arabian for $800,000." The 10th Diamond Horseshoe Tie Ball was held in the Grand Trianon Ballroom of the Beverly Wilshire Hotel. The Ambassador of "Free China" was honored by the Americanism Educational League at the same time as the police chief of L.A., Ed Davis, was given the "Outstanding American of the Year Award" by the L.A. Philanthropic Foundation, also at a hotel meal. Carroll Righter, astrologer to the stars, was giving crisp advice to the readers of *Society West:* "Geminis, public charities are good outlets to bring you prestige.

Moonchild, enjoy some very happy romantic moments. Be Happy. Scorpio, charm everyone by that special warmth that you so easily can turn on. Sagittarius, some very happy romantic moments." (Moonchild and Sagitarius might collaborate, it seems.) And Pisces? "Society interests are now excellent for you. Meet the finest possible persons."

In the same issue, Doug Gross and Stanley Garner are thanked for hosting "a Saturday night luau that was more Hawaiian than Hawaii itself. Some stayed at the party until dawn threw a pink frown across the forehead of the night." Rachel Anderson's poodle, Agnes Anderson, also gave a party. "Beware of Rachel, she can lick you to death, and almost did when her hostess gifts of pure red beef arrived." A Ms. Wonderful Award was given to Rita Hayworth. An artist is described with the words, "In the very near future his price will at least double or triple." Malibu Navy officers dressed in female Hawaiian garb for another party, "each a sight to behold." And Ruth Carter Stapleton, the President's sister, discussed her need for "Unconditional Love for All Humanity" at a conference sponsored by the Association for Holistic Health.

And that's just for November. But somebody seems to know what all this pure red poodle beef means, for buried in the newspaper is one more item, entitled, "Nostalgic Night in Old California"—"An Evening in Old California dinner dance, dancing, Mexican food, in an early California hacienda like Daddy's . . . *All proceeds are directed to the Emphysema Foundation.*"

Joke from Cyrano's on the Sunset Strip: "My wife ran away with my best friend, and I really miss him."
Headline: MISS UNIVERSE ARREST
Los Angeles (AP) November 9
Miss Universe of 1961 was being held for $50,000 bail yesterday

following her second arrest on a drug-related charge in a week.

Police said Constance Meyer, 36, was arrested and booked for investigation of possessing cocaine Wednesday by Hollywood police she summoned to her apartment, saying she was being harassed by a former boyfriend.

Years ago, my favorite literary item from L.A. was the news in a Hollywood gossip column that "Natalie Wood will be playing the title role in the film to be made from the book 'Arma Gedden.' " There are real people playing the Apocalypse out there (starring Pock Alypse?).

"Are you a Pisces?" asked the woman gas station attendant. "Because I can't hack it with Pisceans."

"Could you check my oil?"

"You're really into checking your oil, aren't you? I'm a Capricorn. Only certain men please me. You're half a quart low."

"What do I need?"

She stared. "Like most men around here, you need to get your act together."

A sincere-type actress and model said to me at the Troubador, where she was looking for . . . looking for . . . looking for what might happen in a discotheque, but she had heard of this ancient, ten-year-old rock showplace: "I believe in karma, that's my religion, whatever you do comes back to you double or triple. If you rip people off, you get ripped off. But if you're just nice to people, they'll be wonnerful to you. And you won't necessarily have to fuck them, but you'll want to."

The nearsighted bandit demands, "Stick 'em up! . . . Are they up?" In the same way, the proud Angeleno announces, "You love it here, it's a wonderful whole place! . . . *Don't you?*"

Sometimes, driving in the rain down one of the older

streets, the toy houses and decor make it look, through the working wipers, like the pages of a children's book, tattered and abandoned in a summer house. It could be real for the people who live there, but something nostalgic, sad, and colorful is emerging through the aging of Los Angeles. History finally begins to exist; or at least a wistful child's history.

The hood of my car flew up on the freeway. I pulled blindly off the road. I tied it with rope. I searched in low gear for someone to repair it. WELDING SHOP. I headed in. A bull-necked crewcut old man with huge mandible gloves said, "Naw, I don't do car work."

"What am I going to do?"

I started for my car. I was lost in a part of the Valley which was as far from home as any place I could imagine.

"Okay, let me get at that job," he said.

He welded a new catch onto the hood. He charged me a couple of dollars. I thanked him. After his griping and complaining that it was not his work, he said: "If you can't do a favor for someone, you might as well not do it."

"The favor?"

"You might as well," he said.

I understood the generous thought if not the language. The welder was a human being in his gloves and mask and asbestos armor; he was the knight guardian of my safety; I was a voyager in need.

Los Angeles pioneered Los Angeles-style architecture. The tautology conceals some moderate wisdom. This country is fantasy and need. So there are skyscrapers of glass and aluminum lining Wilshire Boulevard, the children of Bauhaus, and there also are drive-ins built like hamburgers, sundaes, ships, Japanese temples, and seraglios. People live in grand pianos, giant Hansel-and-Gretel huts, petit Trianons and Bavarian castles. What seems more authentic and sweet, the redwood spidery constructions sometimes found clinging to steep canyon walls, is really borrowed from that other state which we can call Northern California. The true architecture is horizontal, the freeway system. Pasadena has millionaire tracts, like Shaker Heights, Ohio. The Valley has Levittowns. Malibu has modified fishing huts for movie stars and electronic millionaires along the ocean. Bob Dylan built a two-million-dollar hideaway on the beach, with instructions that he wanted a living room large enough for a horse to canter through, but then had to debate proprietorship with his wife. Divorce ends most living arrangements down here, not death or horses. There is a tract, Brentwood, Truesdale Heights, some such names, where the houses are mostly Greek temples. I visited one where a sentimental New York producer of soft porn kept a floodlight between the Doric columns, shining on a Central Park bench kept in a cage, his pet memory.

An actor friend of mine puts his income into his house. Here a tennis court (spaghetti western), there a hot tub and Jacuzzi added to the swimming pool (taco commercial). Mud slides wear into his miniature eucalyptus grove. The native redwoods are disappearing. The eucalyptus, a handsome and useless tree, smelling strong and cool, was brought from the East with the thought it might be useful as wood. It is useful for pleasure; that's enough.

The widow of a famous actor rents out their house, and lives off the income in a palatial camper in which she cruises from estate to estate, until her dead husband's friends ask her to please park elsewhere awhile. She keeps hair drier, electric coffee maker, stereo console, a whole discount shop of appliances in her camper, and hooks up to the electric security gates. She has not yet decided what to do with her life. So far, she might write. She has written the first chapter of her autobiography, describing her sexual experiences before and after the funeral. One week makes an interesting story; I tell her, reading the manuscript, I'm not sure it's a full-length book. "What do you know about commerce?" she asks me.

The architectural spaghetti of Los Angeles—all right, call it bouillabaisse in elegant Westwood and Beverly Hills and Malibu—makes living there a form of desolate theater if you too are not a star. If all the world's a stage, and all of us merely players, what profiteth a man to be merely an extra? To drive a clunker, to live in a tract or decaying section of Hollywood if you're older than twenty-eight, does not feel marvelous. You are supposed to feel marvelous among the bougainvillea, the palms, the Mercedes-Benz, the expense account dining. (Sign on a Mexican restaurant: WE SERVE LUNCHO.) The sense of theater here is traditional. Nathanael West wrote that paper has been made to look like wood, wood like rubber, rubber like steel, steel like cheese. That was a generation ago. Alive now, he might report that hairdressers look like movie producers and, amazingly, it has become chic for movie producers to look like hairdressers, psychiatrists like surfers.

To avoid Forest Lawn, Nathanael West's ashes were scattered over the coastline. This great chronicler of the Los Angeles bizarre seems to have sprouted lots of little Westlings. Every Hollywood writer, during his period of unemployment, writes a Hollywood novel. During one of the writers' strikes, an ardent proletarian leader in cashmere sweater and tailored Dacs pounded his desk at a meeting and cried out the agony of the Workers: "My fellow craftsmen! I happen to know there are still writers in this town earning less than a thousand dollars a week!"

So if you are feeling marvelous and up for all this play, the Theater of Hallucinatory Reality makes every day a fantasy feast carried into reality, like a dream remembered, or more precisely, like a movie. Lives unreel on endless tape loops. A flat of a Paris café is knocked down, and Nevada appears behind it—fine! A man in a three-piece suit drives home in his native-born compact car from his law office, puts on his leathers and jumps on his BMW cycle and roars down the Sunset Strip—he has any life he chooses! Occasionally a volcano explodes, as one did at Pompeii; the depression in aerospace at Lockheed, or a no-hit year in the stock market, when the bankers rip out the rugs, tends to slow things down for a moment or two. A few private clubs or discotheques close. Others always open.

Los Angeles is in some ways the mobile version of Manhattan. There is a desire for richness, variety, pleasure, the invention of self in an image which will surely come clear some day. It is the place where the automobile is treated like the cow in India. It is also a holy place of the human spirit, as India is holy—holy for suffering, holy as devils are holy, damned by passionately stubborn and slippery will. Angelenos may not have read Goethe's *Faust*, but they are looking to make a deal with the devil. Every night can be *Walpurgisnacht.* Every man can dance with a witch, every woman find a sorcerer someplace (maybe only a tennis pro or a hairdresser).

"One always begins to forgive a place as soon as it's left behind," someone says in one of Dickens's novels. But I haven't left Los Angeles behind; I still go there; I don't have to forgive it. I have gone through my horror to find some love for this place which will never be a city. I found a welder who fixed the hood of my car although this was not his job.

Desert and mountain, sea and plain, splendor of landscape are preserved beneath the tar of industry and population. The portmanteau word "slurb" describes the post-urban ooze which flows over what used to be a tiny Spanish settlement. And yet, like the gypsy girl in Tennessee Williams's play *Camino Real,* Los Angeles seems to regain its virginity with each full moon. When the smog clears, and the mountains shine in the reflection of the Pacific, and hope springs eternal in the breasts of the orphan sons and daughters who came to California, choosing new names and identities and roles and futures—not so much making a new past for themselves, as liars might do, but simply wiping out the past—we are all virgins filled with expectation once more. We are a city of Angels, holding the demons at bay. And if any devils find their way through our protective network of highways, we can always solve the problem by naming them angels, too.

L.A. MINI SUPERETTE
Gas, Food, Tums
OPEN 24 HOURS A DAY!
(Closed Midnight to 7 A.M.)

3
San Francisco: The City That Asks if You Came

The story is told that a Mill Valley video freak commune decided to make the bread for some new equipment with a little advanced, underground, commercial, sell-out short subject. Participatory democracy means you never have to say, "I'm sorry, I'd rather deal dope than rip off Allen Funt." So they dressed a woman in the compleat nun's habit and installed her at the San Francisco International Airport, where she was greeted at the gate for the hip, cheap midnight PSA flight from L.A. by a rabbi who began by chastely kissing her. The video crew filmed audience response as the rabbi embraced her sweetly. He put his hand under her habit. They began to struggle. She was gasping. Her cowl was knocked awry. Also his tie. They were both panting and biting, and his tongue was in her mouth, darting in and out, as she bent backward and eventually tumbled to the vinyl-marble floor, and they rolled around in an ecstasy of Welcome to San Francisco while the hidden cameras rolled.

Allen Funt time in the counterculture. Tongues, zippers, cowls, pink folds and crevices undulating.

Well, the people streamed by without noticing.

Finally, one very straight citizen, maybe an insurance executive just in from a bit of desert sun, bent over the ecumenical thumping forms where they lay, tapped the pseudo-nun on the shoulder, and asked, *"Did you come?"*

Despite encroachments of smog from Oakland and high rises from Manhattan, San Francisco remains a name and place apart from other American places and names. Narcissistic, yes; but sexually narcissistic. Another American metropolis, drilling subways, crowding highways, yes; but with a certain juice and languor to its making out and making do. The time of the flower children is over—partly because everyone believes in being turned-on now. The police joke with the whores as of old, they tease the transvestites, they laugh along with the tourists at the parade of post-Cockettes near the Castro Theater at midnight on weekends, they don't beat them up as much as they do in my ancestral Cleveland. There is a Polk Street bar called the White Swallow, located near Hard On Leathers and other shoppes and oases whose signals remain to be decoded. The jeans in the windows of the men's shops face the front with their backs. Perhaps the structure of that sentence is inverted, too. A friend, a proctologist, is writing a book about anal intercourse which should be entitled, *Above and Behind the Call of Duty.* (He sees lots of problems, and is thinking of changing his practice to dermatology or psychiatry—something more comfortable for his riper years.) Hip Sheriff Hongisto introduced a gay minister to serve the gay community in the county jail.

Police, real estate promoters, and big-city thugs are never

quite Gilbert & Sullivan characters, or even lovable rogues from *Guys and Dolls,* but Veblenian marginal differentiation shows its power in San Francisco. So it's a big American city, true—but not just another big American city. Many visitors and transplants grind their teeth and hate it. It doesn't solve a fellow's problems. It can be a zap of mother's milk straight into the eyes, blindingly sweet. The Chamber of Commerce Tourist Bureau's gulls, cable cars, Golden Gate Bridge, and romantic fog tend to zap hometown kids straight in the liver, providing instant hepatitis, or at least a jaundiced gaze. The town is being stripmined for movie-of-the-week atmosphere. Disney discovers crookedest-street-in-the-world. The Ford Times borrows Picturesque Telegraph Hill. The Gray Line ships in busloads of chiropractors with aching backs for a dose of female impersonation (Finocchio's) or here's-where-the-stars-got-their-start (Purple Onion).

San Francisco is not Positano or Acapulco. They are tired, too. But despite media overload, despite its being fed into the great international media meat-grinder, and coming out Hilton Hamburger and Fisherman's Wharf link sausage, San Francisco remains something of what people have always thought about it. While New York and Paris seem to be yearning to become larger versions of Cleveland, and Cleveland is becoming Detroit, San Francisco remains mysteriously itself. This may last for our lifetime.

One day an old friend came to visit for the first time. It happened to be the season of the Chinese New Year, and the streets were filled with costumes, dragons, papier-mâché, firecrackers, and clanking bands dancing like segmented metal caterpillars. The day had been sunny and dry, with the parks occupied by easy strollers. I said this was a city for strolling, and we strolled. The Mime Troupe performed its guerilla theater, with a medieval pope portrayed by a beautiful male actress. A clone of Bobby Shields, the genial whiteface, did his fantastic energy-raising acrobatics in Union Square. A time-lag rock band set up in the Panhandle for an audience of speed freaks who thought it was 1967 again.

It happened that night that my friend had a meal in one of the Italian family-style restaurants on upper Grant, along with a Japanese opera troupe, which rose after the spumoni to sing "Oh! Susanna" in Japanese, in order to show their appreciation. Then my friend fell into conversation with a pretty woman, who described herself as an actor and sex researcher. They discussed the theater. They discussed science. She said good-bye to the group she had come with and they went for a cappuccino at La Tosca, continuing their getting-to-know-you joint arias. Two cappuccinos on the leather banks of La Tosca. Little flutterings in the heart and elsewhere. She took him home with her that night.

The next day my friend asked me with a certain incredulity, "Is it always like this here?"

"Not every day," I was forced to admit. "On Sunday, for example, I drive my daughter to Sunday school. And Chinese New Year is over soon. Next month, I think."

But for some who come to San Francisco, Chinese New Year never ends, despite the alcoholism and breakdown rates, the busing and ghetto issues, the complacent hustle of city politics. It's possible to treat San Francisco as a continuous costume party, Halloween-by-the-bay, and amazingly enough—the flower-child spasm was partly about this—some manage to make of Halloween a way of life. It's not real, but it really happens. San Francisco is not authentic, but it would be genocide to say it isn't as it is. The market for antique funny clothes, outer-space brooms, and witches' brew, seems nearly inexhaustible.

Here is a birthday party at Sally Stanford's humorously posh New Orleans-brothel glass-and-crossword-Tiffany restaurant on the bay in Sausalito. The fest cost thousands. Young Lenny Norton, twenty-one, ex–car parker, was honoring his lawyer, Neil Murphy, dope lawyer, just turning thirty. Oysters flown west, steaks, girls in various stages of stoned and groovy silence, pink and chartreuse sweet liquids; and pilots, lawyers, groupies, coaches, rugby buddies, and even a few proud parents of the businessmen. Lenny's mom and dad, glad that their son the dealer could afford to spend a couple-three thousand on a little birthday party, walked about in their Macy's groove-clothes and said, "Yes, Lenny has a good head for business. Yes, Lenny bought us a little house in El Cerrito, plus some income property in Oakland. Yes, we're Lenny's mom and pop, man. Right on."

Lenny was wearing hotpants, full pancake makeup, dark red Cockette lipstick, and, resting on his skinny arms, the two girls he was planning to ball later. Sally Stanford herself, the ancient madam now playing at crone's career, beamed over the money she was making and poured champagne. A satisfying fiscal popping filled the air under the chandeliers.

I don't want you to think this chic orgy, with all the good food and drink and beautiful girls and men grown rich and dramatic in the dope trade was actually very rowdy and joyous. Everybody was too stoned to do much in the social line. But I enjoyed the fish and meat proteins and a cholesterol dessert. In the john two chauffeurs were discussing the virtues of Cessnas and Beechcrafts of various models in making the run up the coast from Baja. The Staff Headquarters of the Dope Air Force, a combination mercy and Mafia and general teenage rip-off operation, are in Sausalito. More planes than most nations with seats at the U.N.; the largest private air force on a war footing since Mike Nichols gathered his fleet for *Catch-22*. The unzipped pilots, relieving themselves of early champagne ballast, didn't stop their professional murmuring just because I happened to be standing there alongside. "What if I were a narc?" I asked the crew-cut one.

He looked at me and said to the other, "I think the radar screen just made it easier. They're overconfident." And he shook himself dry and free, twenty-eight, a veteran of Viet Nam, cool as Kool-Aid.

On the way out, a desperate group of tourists from a nearby table clutched my arm. They were ready to weep with frustration and desire. They watched a hundred freaks gobbling up caviar, French wines, steaks, oysters, cool, so cool, and these Latter-Day-Saint tourists from Salt Lake City felt that I, perhaps the eldest member of that crowd, was their last hope for salvation short of the return of bearded Joseph Smith. *"Who are those people?"* one hissed, his fundamentalist talons scrabbling against my corduroy jacket.

"The strike committee from Pacific Telephone," I said, and they nodded. They too always knew San Francisco would be like this.

No picturesque weirdness means that San Francisco escapes being an American city, with all the problems of an American city, while it also has some of the provincial, exempted charm of other hilly and provincial port cities, such as Leningrad, Marseilles, Naples, and Haifa, which live freed from the responsibilities of capitals—Moscow, Paris, Rome, Jerusalem—and therefore preserve something traditional, both highly colored by the sea and less hectic in the culture. Once, thanks to the gold rush, San Francisco had an intense hour in the sun. Mainland China Trade Stores have opened with soft commercial smiles in the wake of the various presidential China spectaculars, and perhaps San Francisco could have another gold rush if shipping and trade really begins to shuttle between the old opium states and the West Coast.

Whether or not the town becomes Venice again, a window to elsewhere, it shares certain household frets in common with all other American centers—race, poverty, welfare, slums, freeways, school systems, smog, the resentments of Middle America, the rage of deprived America, the flight of money from the central city. It is not exempt from the times. Despite all the money, power, shipping, unions, major corporations, it's still a consumer's easy garden city, a terrarium in America.

But gardens, as everyone knows, are filled with worms and other beasties. The green hides violence, red in tooth and claw. They fire at the President here. And Dan White, a disgruntled nice boy, ex-fireman, ex-policeman, ex-supervisor, crawled through a window of City Hall to murder Mayor Moscone and Harvey Milk, the homosexual supervisor. And was given a wristslap sentence by a San Francisco jury which found he was just a nice boy led astray by concern for his city, an I.Q. not equal to his aspirations, and overindulgence in Twinkies, causing sugar panic and psychiatric testimony.

The barker at The Condor in North Beach looks like the star of a teevee series pilot called "The Young Dentist," but on speed. He is skinny, sharp-featured, very fast, and suggests slurping eroticism while doing busy work with his teeth. His hair is as short as an Orange County football coach's, yet you don't see the scalp through it. He paces back and forth with methamphetamine rancor, chanting, "Come on in, organic sex! Sex is the best aphrodisiac! Come on in, all topless and bottomless college coeds!" He doesn't specify the school.

The Jesus people on the sidewalk outside The Condor are no longer shooting, sniffing, or smoking; they have found Jesus, or at least Pat Boone. They have long hair. Their complexions look up at their scalps reproachfully, if complexions could look, saying, *Shampoo a little.* Keep clean, a little shampoo isn't dirty. One is selling Jesus Now, with a headline: MOSHE FINDS CHRIST, LEARNS LOVE. "It's free, it's true," whispers a girl in a granny dress. She is thrusting the paper into hands which promptly litter. A long-haired young man, square wire glasses, like a lobotomized Harvard kid, is crying out with fixed Teutonic smile: "Abstain from filth!"

Meanwhile, he too is handing out leaflets which fall to the street from the nerveless fingers of tourists.

"Aw, knock it off," says the pacing Young Dentist. "I'm working this doorway, not you, kids."

"Knock off this abomination!" cries the ambassador from Jesus-in-San Rafael. "Here, read the Truth as we learned it!"

The battle between the drag-em-off-the-street barker at the topless bar and the Jesus freaks. "Be saved by Jee-zuz!"

"Get some sex! It's organic!"

"Christ will save you!"

"For Christ's sake, get the fuck out of here.!

"We'll do what we can for you. Jesus loves you!"

"Tell you what you can do for me, go across the street and let Jesus love the Garden of Allah."

It was a countdown between the short-haired businessmen selling sex and the long-haired freaky Christians selling salvation. Some leather-jacketed allies of The Condor gathered about the barker to consider extreme unction; that is, kicks in rear, shoves over curb. But in the typical distortion brought about by the media, the fact of my standing there, gaping like a journalist, changed history. They said, "Aw, fuck," and went inside to drink and enjoy bottomless dancing, not living up to their promise. The Jesus freaks eventually climbed into a blue VW bus and drove back to their commune in the Haight, where they get high on Christ and brown rice. They mix the traditions.

A few weeks later they were busted for housing runaways. Heroin is still sold in adjacent doorways.

When I packed my wagon and hit the trail from New York in 1960, I had plans to spend a year in Friscoville, where there had been happy times on a visit in 1957—Alan Ginsberg, the Co-Existence Bagel Bar, Mad Alex the Talker, Bob Kaufman the poet ("Notes Found at the Tomb of the Unknown Draft Dodger"), my brother beatniks getting beaten around the head by Officer Bigarani on upper Grant. By the time I came to stay, the beat movement was frazzled away by a combination of media overload, changing times, and natural wear. Guitars were being traded in for washer-dryers, wine for grass, and the long somnolence which would suddenly erupt in 1966–67 (flower children, Haight-Ashbury, "we are the children of the beats") needed a certain incubation period. Still, doorways and chess bars were filled with patient dissemblers, awaiting the next call. San Francisco was a town in which no one had to decide whether or not to open the windows. Good working. A host of lawyers, doctors, architects, post-analysands were deciding not to get rich but to get happy on the Bay. A nice place to idle away the rest of the century.

Then, around 1965–66 . . . No, let's name the night. On the night when I heard the Jefferson Airplane in the Matrix on Fillmore—amplified? what's this? Speak a little louder, I can't hear you—it was clear that a new implosion had occurred, and explosion would follow. The cybernetic revolution had hit the beat guitar. It was as if every washer-dryer in the universe was churning out its Bendix slurp-and-roll. I was, I'll admit it—*charmed.*

The rest is the history of the micro-moment. The primal horde discovered Levi's. Old Kronos was dealing at the corner of Haight and Ashbury. Poster art became visual rock and roll; the youthquake became a market. Both Bechtel Corporation and the Greening of America industry had their headquarters here. Into the great media machine was fed the hope and dream of a time. "I'm not putting down the Viet Nam War," declared a retired activist from Berkeley, no longer interested in politics, tuned in, turned on, dropped out, and cured like beef jerky. "After all, Viet Nam brought us all together, so it was a real good thing."

And in the flash of a season, it was Mafia-hip, MGM groovy, a style for every college and big city in the country. A revolution, a fashion, and an industry all in one. The bands were no longer playing for free in the park, they were playing for fortunes for Bill Graham Presents. The Diggers stopped serving their buffalo stew in the Panhandle. Emmett Grogan wrote his memoirs for Little, Brown. Post-hip in San Francisco is like post-beat: there are still people in doorways, hiding out, waiting for the next movement. The town staggers along, looking for its next movement. There are those who swear that when it happens they won't tell anyone. But if they don't, will it be a Movement? Guru poets on the Great Highway, beating old coffee cans till their heads spin, expanding their consciousness and destroying their eardrums, are they really a Movement? One says, "I'm a Countercultural Biggie," and maybe he is, but the traffic whooshes by and not many stop to receive the message. The Jews for Jesus Country Western band chants its latest hit:

I knew Jesus
Before he was a Gentile

On Haight Street a strung-out speed-freak in dirty denims stopped a passerby and invited him to her pad. "I may not be a flower child anymore," she said enticingly, "but come with me anyway. Have you ever had a real pig?"

No, she was not really a flower child anymore. Haight Street for awhile was a teenage slum; then a speed-and-heroin-real-estate hell, dropped all the way out. Now it is being revived as a Madison Avenue or Union Street for unisex speculators, middle-class blacks, and a few fix-it young couples with adventure in their hearts.

The special story about San Francisco may be that it is a place to drop out while not absolutely dropping out. A former graduate student and mad bomber, fled to Canada after trying to end the war in Viet Nam by ending the Bank of America, now dwells at relative peace with himself in Bernal Heights. He confessed, regretted, returned, did a bit of prison, had his skull fractured in the showers by a patriotic felon, recovered, wears a steel plate in his head, and now works for Sparkies, delivering packages. He has a pretty wife. "That's not the way," he says about bombing. The urban-rural slum, an interracial community on the hilly slope of Bernal, now gives him a home. There are even unpaved streets, and chickens, and backyard gardens, plus coffee houses and theater groups and action art galleries. Despite his periodic headaches and dizzy spells, life isn't too bad. The doctor says he won't necessarily develop epilepsy.

A former hotshot editor, once quick and randy, now reformed, ecstatic, transformed, says calmly about his projects for the future: "I'll neither make plans for the future nor not make plans. I'll neither do things nor not do things. I'm learning about my body and soul these days, but I don't care if I'm really learning, either." His smile is beatific. His walk is smooth. His heart is pure.

A former Manhattan women's liberation activist has come to San Francisco and is losing the struggle against her sexist hang-ups. She still raises her consciousness at consciousness-raising meetings, and exchanges clitoral know-how with her sisters, but more and more she tends to regard her husband as a human being. She can't fight the town.

The habits of transferees from major corporations—insurance, banking, real estate, conglomerates left over from the great mergers of the sixties, advertising agency managers and media organizers—are known for a certain inevitable life direction. The pattern can be predicted. They arrive in their eastern J. Press or Brooks Brothers neatness, look around with hauteur at the gray-haired, long-haired groovers, and they swear on their honor: "Well, I won't wear the vest. I'll wear the three-piece suit without the vest. But that's as far as I'll go."

"Don't swear," I tell them, "it's impious."

Pretty soon some little State University of New York at Buffalo dropout, now waitressing at the Trident or MacArthur Park while she "gets her shit together," begins to recount her life story: "Neil broke my heart three weeks ago. Maybe I'm not a woman, just a little girl, but my heart breaks, too. So three weeks ago, when Neil broke my heart, I decided—"

And Mr. Media Transferee is nodding, nodding, nodding. Tell me more.

A few weeks later, as he sits there still nodding, he is telling Neil's ex-old lady "I chose a lower-paying job to live out here, because six months ago, when my wife broke my heart, I knew I couldn't stand that uptight scene anymore—"

It's the Sports Car Menopause all the way. What looked like the Groovy Horde, maddened flower ghouls and pagan flits, is now, in the flash of a season, just Standard American to Mr. Media Transferee. He may not have qualified as a card-carrying teenager in twenty years. That's no reason for not changing his life.

I speak with due diffidence as one of his spiritual cousins. I have lived in Cleveland, New York, Paris, Port-au-Prince, Detroit, and New York—a tipsy itinerary, I'll admit—with way stations in Havana, Key West, and Fort Bragg—and until I came to San Francisco, I always dreamed of eventually settling in Paris, the City of Light, where I had spent idle student and dreamy bohemian years. I would be a stroller on two sides of the river. In the capital of misery and the paradise of hope would I dwell forever, just like Villon, Carco, and Jean-Paul Sartre.

So when I arrived to pass a season in San Francisco, having sublet my flat in Greenwich Village, it was just to do a job. I was having a play produced at the old Actors' Workshop. Hmm, so this is Frisco, I thought.

Two weeks later I phoned back to New York and told my tenants to keep the place. I was staying. I left my clothes there so long they came back into style. My blue suit, fit only to wear at Stalin's funeral, is now just right for the midnight show, *Reefer Madness,* and the Cockettes' Sylvester's newest comeback stage presentation. I still have things in storage with various friends around Manhattan, though I now recognize the law which states that a loan for more than a year is a gift. Never mind those lampshades, Japanese prints, and wide pants, Marcus: they're yours.

Why? Why have I sold out Paris, abandoned Manhattan?

I'm trying to say it's fun here. The town has really succeeded in limiting high-rise development. The morning and evening tides really wash the pollution out of the bay, so that we dolphins can scream and swim in the chill waters. The TransAmerica Pyramid wasn't so ugly as I thought it would be when I harangued the Board of Supervisors about destroying North Beach. A few years earlier, in another great battle, I was co-chairman of the Anti-Digit-Dialing League, along with S. I. Hayakawa. Well, we've got nothing but digits now. You can't win them all. We voted a city-wide initiative against the Viet Nam War. We cleaned up the oil slick on the beaches. We are not a sweet garden separated from the real world, like Italy. It feels here as if we are living real life, only in a more advanced stage. Italy may feel the same way about itself and the habit of political kneecapping and murder.

For example, take Project Artaud and Project One, warehouses to the people. They were defunct real estate disaster areas, gloomy brick and space in perishing parts of the town. "What is valuable?" asked a few revolutionary innovators. Well, for one thing, bricks, space, windows, doors, rooms, roofs—these things we love. The gloom we can do away with. Artists need space, and so do galleries, filmmakers, literary magazines, free schools, consciousness-raising women's groups, revolutionary action societies, Zen meditators, musicians (especially rock musicians, who tend to shiver foundations and send neighbors to the emergency telephone); gropers and rappers need space, embryo feeling orgs need space—people need space. Dollars per square foot are real issues. Project Artaud formed a cooperative, including even automobile repair gurus in the courtyard, to take over the moribund buildings and give them to the people, spelled The People, at minimum rents plus occasional basic metaphysic sessions. This is countercultural real estate ferment, and it works. Project One followed Project Artaud, just as a few years ago, the *Free Press* followed the *Berkeley Barb*. Home organic food bakeries, yogurteries, leather connivers, all the enterprises of the countercultural ferment found an amiable environment south of Market in an old blue-collar, light-industry, heavy-trucking part of town. One winter they even had a reading by Yevtushenko, with mobs waiting to support a new concept in square footage.

When Project One became valuable, the owners decided to put out the artists and put in real people. It's a familiar story.

Countercultural San Franciscans sometimes think they are all of San Francisco, somewhat in the state of mind of the

Dupont executive of the thirties, who refused to sponsor a Sunday afternoon radio program on the grounds that: "On Sunday afternoon everyone is playing polo." In fact, San Francisco is middle-class strivers, union people, dockmen, straight insurance clerks, Chinese and Japanese immigrants looking to make out okay, a large black and Chicano population—the usual mix of a great American city. All the minority of the turned-on do is what is most important: give the city its tone and reputation, its style in the breeze of the mind. The flower children, the traditional bohemians, and the polo players are merely the minority which sets the tone. Out in Daly City and South San Francisco, in the Sunset and the Richmond, there are the standard-sized okay Americans who attend services at the First Church of Christ Discounter (All Prayers Guaranteed) and think Ché Guevara was somebody's girlfriend. They are decent people who lead decent lives and read the *San Francisco Examiner,* flagship of the Hearst empire.

But a stroller, looking for other news of the city, might have found, say, the Physicians Exchange Pharmaceutical Service (PEPS) storefront office on Powell along the cable car tracks. Inside, instead of doctors or clerks, there were cots with freaks sleeping, a few drug house magazines, and nothing much happening. Every once in a while I'd hang around. They'd give me coffee and I'd feel so good. "Say," I might ask, "what are you chaps *really—*"

The shrugs were beginning.

"—really, really doing?"

The shrugs were continuing.

"Don't tell me, I don't want to know," I added.

"Okay, you're a friend mumble-mumble," they'd say. They were all lank, cadaverous young men with beards, like young Howard Hugheses fresh out of San Jose State. There were bunches of pencils in their pockets. They would write little things down, sleep a while, then write some more. They didn't speak much to each other, in the fashion of family, as if they communicated by smell and felt no need of conversation. They had the electronic genius look, and old laundry smell. They read *Mad Magazine* and the underground press, and only occasionally I noticed a ravishing pink blonde girl waking up on the cot in the back room.

"I didn't hear a word," I said in response to an explanation I couldn't make out.

Somehow it was nice to laze and gefuffle in that room, until one day it was closed and sealed BY ORDER OF U.S. MARSHAL and the beards and cots were gone. And now it's rented to a gift shop.

Who, what, where, why, how? Weathermen, underground press service, dope exchange, con rip-off freaks, kids playing send-away-for-samples? A pure exercise of style?

Really don't know.

Frisco days and nights. Paris used to be like this. I remember the pretenders to the throne of Holy Russia, printing posters, plotting their White revolution; probably they still have an office in Montmartre, three-generation refugees from Lenin.

Once I thought I saw the pink blonde girl on a cable car, but I couldn't catch her to ask what happened, where our friends were meeting now. She was rubbing her chin in the collar of her suede coat. Perhaps that was a signal to me. I rubbed my own chin in response, but she just rode the cable car up Hyde Street to the summit. Maybe I chose the wrong signal.

Who are those other ghostly figures walking down Russian, Nob, and Telegraph hills at dawn? Those samurai knights shrouded in mist are the stockbrokers, who must be at work by 7:00 A.M. to keep up with Wall Street. Due to the time change, when it's three o'clock in the morning in the dark night of the soul of Manhattan, it's only midnight in San Francisco. Bill Graham, now fifty, is an ancient San Francisco rock millionaire. Soon he'll be starting a new career, a new marriage, new family; watch and see. It's only midnight in the dark night of the soul. The girl from PEPS may be haunting someplace, too, waiting for the next federal padlock. (Or maybe she's hijacking a plane someplace, holding it for ransom, getting bills in small denominations and trying to decide whether to ask for the halibut or the roast beef dinner.) It does sometimes seem as if the heist artists have more style in San Francisco: the check-writer who keeps buying Bentleys (his psychiatrist says he has a Bentley fixation), the would-be rapist who rejected his victim at the last minute, morosely describing her as a ball-breaker. A woman named Gloria Something sued the transit authority, charging that a cable car accident transformed her into a nymphomaniac, and a San Francisco jury awarded her a judgment of $50,000 for her psychic wounds. Suggested headline: GLORIA SICS TRANSIT. Later a local porn producer made a film inspired by this tragic episode in the history of transportation.

The city is not immune to all the American troubles of violence, spite, and anomie. A young actress, raped at knifepoint in the hall of her apartment house, proceeded afterward to trudge upstairs to her flat, telephone her boyfriend, and say, "A funny thing just happened to me. We could use it in an improvisation . . ."

Another well-known social lady had the following conversation with a rapist who invaded her house and forced herself and her children to parade nude in front of him:

RAPIST: (as she reported the conversation to the police) Gosh, you're beautiful.

LADY: Well, I'm a little overweight these days.

The rapist thought about it, then raped the maid while his

accomplices held the family at bay. The rapist returned to the lady.

RAPIST: Would you like me to rape you, too?

LADY: No, thanks.

The rape team then gathered up a few baubles and left. The lady reported to her friends that the leader stopped raping the maid when his accomplices approached. "And I think that shows a glimmer of sensitivity in the man, don't you?"

I don't mean to imply that random violence, drug fiends, the assassination of political leaders, and sexual tensions are just cute in San Francisco. But they sometimes seem to be different. When I was slugged on the neck by a disappointed stock market investor, and knocked sprawling into Montgomery Street, his first question as I came up was why Fannie Mae, Federal National Mortgage, hadn't lived up to its early promise. It had gone up, then it went down, then up again, and now back down. How can you count on a stockbroker who recommends a stock like that? I wasn't a stockbroker, but I deserved to be hit because I couldn't explain it to him, either. I think it showed a glimmer of sensitivity in the man that he didn't stab me, too.

I didn't mind getting married, because my wife told me to go on walking in North Beach. It's good for the legs, wind, and cardio-vascular system, and therefore the heart; my soul is aired in fogs salted by the sea, peppered by human spices; and although not the same—I wasn't what you'd call *prowling* anymore—I took a new perspective on the tiny implosions of animus and entertainment in the Barbary Coast, the International Settlement, on Broadway, up and down Columbus and Grant where ghosts, shades, artists, tourists, pimps and would-be pimps, dealers and dealees, marks and targets wandered the time-lag evening.

For example, Ken Rand, proprietor of the Minimum Daily Requirement café, had a little problem with the speed freaks, junkies, whores, two-baggie businessmen, runaways, and pouting poets who hang out without buying more than coffee. One evening he just got fed up with this near-albino lady, very ugly, about twenty-two; huge doughnut buttocks, whitish hair a little darker at the roots, complexion of blah and bump, about forty pounds overweight, poorly distributed. She looked like a girlfriend of Papa Boy Duvalier, I thought (I had just come home from a stroll in Port-au-Prince). She was talking too much, and she wasn't talking to anyone visible. Ken approached her with his neat, mustachioed suave (he attended various eastern schools and enjoys his scene with a certain Charles River hauteur). "All right, Marlene, you should go someplace else now."

She said, "Unh."

"Come on, Marlene, give us a rest. Let's move, Marlene. I'll walk you to the door."

"Unh." This was half of unh-unh.

He took her by the elbow, firmly, between several fingers, and urged her forward. She flounced. Shielding half the squeezed, puddled doughnuts, she was wearing some kind of semi-Bermuda shorts and bare feet. His pressure around elbow got through to her, because she was angry, but he walked, still gracious and smiling, as far as the door with her. Whereupon she turned, stared balefully out of eyes that could oink if eyes made oinks, and raised her sweater. Underneath there was nothing. That is, there was plenty, but nothing else. She took a breast and, still fixing Ken with that silent oink, lifted it between suddenly skillful fingers. And shot him a jet of milk straight between the eyes.

Ken closed the MDR and opened the Sand Dollar, a relaxed and elegant seaside restaurant in Stinson Beach, down the coast on Route 1 a few miles from North Beach.

San Francisco: The City That Asks if You Came

I get up in the morning and now it's time once more to go where the city leads me. Now that I'm divorced, I can both stroll and prowl. A piece of strange is San Francisco.

Richard Brautigan is writing a poem about a girl with hair down to her ass, and everybody wants her, and there is Richard Brautigan, lonely with his brandy on the terrace at Enrico's, looking to find the girl he has just written about. The parade of girls with hair down to their asses passes.

I am an anti-guru. I too am sitting there alone, inspired by the sight of Richard Brautigan, but determined not to write a poem about girls with hair down to their asses.

SAN FRANCISCO ANTI-GURU POEM
The anti-guru
Stood on the mountain
Extended his arms to the masses below
  below
    below
      below
and cried
      cried
    cried
  cried:
"Do not follow me!"

4
How the Village of Palm Springs Became P°A°L°M S°P°R°I°N°G°S

Condo is the big word in town.

Palm Springs used to be that sandbox for grown-up millionaires where the boss entertainment was sitting in the sun, counting your ducats, rubbing lotion on your skin, and running down to catch a glimpse of former President Eisenhower wheeling around on his golf cart at the Thunderbird Club. The addresses of the movie stars were *listed* (small town casual) in the phone book. You could hang out with landrich desert gophers and gossip about the Agua Caliente ("Hot Water") Indians, every one of them *very well off*. There was no topless entertainment. Instead, you watched sunsets, sunrises, and date palms.

It was retirement villas for the mature, too rich to be geriatric; safe harbor for Frank Sinatra and his fleet of warplanes. Charlie Farrell, costar with Janet Gaynor in *Seventh Heaven*, took care of athletics at his Racquet Club—strict dress regulations.

Well, no longer. That is, many of these attractions remain —substitute Spiro T. Agnew for Dwight David Eisenhower —but some modern pleasures have drifted across the desert. Discotheques. Book shops. Young folks in bi and monokinis. Runners and joggers. Party people. Funners. The date palms still perform their natural act for curious visitors, but so do honeymooners, relaxed allergists from Cleveland, condominium collectors. Palm Springs has entered the post-Aquarian Age.

It used to be said that the pure dry air was humidified by clouds forming over the densest cluster of swimming pools in the world. Now an occasional wisp of smog comes exploring seepishly over the mountains from the industrial civilization to the west, where the money tends to be born. It used to be that the Hollywood agents who strolled Palm Canyon Drive in their pointy Italian shoes and black silk suits had not been to college. Now they have Harvard degrees, and talk about "auteur theory."

Ah, there was the flying grandmother. There were people who knew Howard Hughes personally, before he grew his fingernails. There was the first laundromat in the world equipped with color television, conceived by an enterprising Agua Caliente Indian Native American. The town was called "the Village." As a booster drove me through the Village, he muttered a subtext of commentary along with the conversation: "Rolls . . . T-Bird . . . Continental . . . Nother Continental . . . Caddy," naming them as we passed. When we parked in Charlie Farrell's Racquet Club lot, he pulled his Corvette between a Bentley and a Continental, gazed up rakishly into my eyes, and whispered, "I sure got a lot of nerve, don't I?"

But enough of sentimental violins. I revisited Palm Springs in what would have been the dead of last winter in the real world, my bags filled with alligator tennis shirts, my hopes of fun turned expectantly to the desert sun.

My hopes did not wait in vain.

The first hint of change came when I checked into the Ingleside Inn, a smallish, elegantish former private estate. It looked familiar, the lot filled with the usual antique and custom wheels, none of your normal transportation in Palm Springs, but then I was handed an informative leaflet entitled "GARBO SLEPT HERE."

Uh-oh.

I feared an uphill struggle. Garbo wants to be alone—is that what they were selling? But I, I, a poor lonely writer, I am too young to be alone. I want song! dance! tennis! sociable gazes from one or several sundried but inwardly humid creatures! Wrought iron portals might suffice for some. I need Ali McGraw, Candy Bergen, even Cybil Shepherd if she will slim down just a little.

They showed me to a villa by the pool which was spacious, charming, unique, and comfortable. It had a fireplace lovingly set with paper, kindling, and logs. I scowled. How can a man be happy alone in such a room? I took out my copies of Albert Camus's *The Myth of Sisyphus,* Kierkegaard's *Either-Or,* and Kevin Starr's *Americans and the California Dream.* Yes, I had already read these books. But I had not read them in Palm Springs, where everything is different. Even the towels are richer and fluffier. Happy in my solitude by the crackling fire with the fluffy towels and the complimentary bowl of fruit supplied by the management to Garbo and me, I read and read.

Two minutes later I jumped up and went to Melvyn's Restaurant and Lounge to catch the action. The food was prepared with care, the drinks generous, the room filled with people whose faces I almost recognized. I ate with quiet dignity, a napkin on my lap, like a mysterious foreign gentleman alone on a holiday. Afterwards, a midnight swim in a pool filled with mysterious foreign ladies on a holiday. A good beginning.

From the air, Palm Springs is a series of sketches drawn by a child's finger in the sandpile—roads, subdivisions, blue blots of pools for cavorting and basking. Then the plane lands, and there is purple sage along the runways at the airport, matching the hair of my Air California stewardess.

The Ingleside Inn has been waked up, like the Sleeping Beauty, by a tough, hip, fast-talking New Yorker, Mel Haber, who has a passion to make it Fun for himself and his guests. He succeeds. Mel is probably metabolically amused, and even liked the automobile accessory business and his first wife, but he *really* loves Melvyn's, his restaurant.

He talked fast and pungently. "The town is full of scammers. I see the great of this world—McQueen, Sinatra, Kirk Kerkorian—and also a giant in the ready-to-wear business, a *giant,* who comes in with this blonde strudel could be his ... not his daughter, his *granddaughter*—he's a giant! I'll tell you one thing right off: everyone's single in Palm Springs. Go to Pal Joey's or Mawby's—those are discotheques, man—to make it official. After eleven o'clock."

(I went. Foreign correspondent flinches before no dangers, even "Mr. Clean and His Clean Machine" at Mawby's.)

(It's official.)

Mel Haber explained how the Ingleside Inn, a little spread of Transylvanian luxury in the desert, became an *In* Inn, with Mel himself the potential subject of a CBS prime time show. "There's a greatness in me. I found it in the hotel-restaurant business of selling charm. I'm just a simple kid from Brooklyn. I got these antique cars, I got this wine cellar, but you know me, I just love this whole scam."

"It's nice. The Jacuzzi twists good. I like it."

"Oh, I got my touches, my subtle little moves. I learned from experience. For example, the matches with the name on it in every suite. 'The Schwartzes.' So the guy goes home and his wife unpacks him and she finds matches—*The Schwartzes! Who were you with, chump?*" Mel shook his head with the wisdom of the hotelier trade. "So now the matches just say *Schwartz.* Plain old just Schwartz, like that. Boom. You can't hang a man for Schwartz."

And he ran to take a call from a visitor who was almost governor of one of our top states, only he lost the election.

I would have rented a bicycle at Mack's Bike Rental for voyages of exploration in the mountain/desert air, but they supplied one at the Ingleside Inn. At the Sunshine Meat, Fish & Liquor Company on South Palm Canyon Drive I found "Freedom Rising," a rock group doing mellow. I found a Fresh Clear Water Catfish dinner at a restaurant whose name I forget. (Notes fell out of pocket on bicycle.) There's lots to do and eat out in what is no longer a tranquil millionaire's rest camp.

A friendly soul from the Convention & Visitors Bureau invited me to lunch and a haircut. We attended a unisexual styling parlor together. I had my first blow-dry job. The last time I had my hair trimmed in a barber shop was ten years ago in Lawrence, Kansas, where I feared lynching otherwise. Normally it's done by devoted squinting good friends. I paid for this service a few months ago, when I picked up a furloughed Trident waitress who was hitchhiking across the Golden Gate Bridge to Sausalito. Out of work, desperate, slim and lovely, and a skilled coiffeuse, she offered to take me home and, for five dollars, give me a haircut I would never forget. She did; I didn't. While she cut my hair she told me about how she was crazy for a member of the '49ers, a prominent football team in the Bay Area, and all she asked of a man is that he be the proud possessor of at least six feet four inches of altitude and two hundred and fifty pounds of amplitude and he was due to arrive any minute. I gave her the five dollars plus my blessing plus I didn't wait to be blown dry.

So maybe it won't be for everybody, but for me a hair job at The Headquarters in the Fashion Mall in Palm Springs made it a real fine special vacation, a shearing experience.

And now a little medley of tunes from Palm Canyon Drive, which is in a bustle of Christmas shopping the year round. The lights in the palm trees give an impression of forever holiday, but this is serious: "We have no quarrel with those who sell for less. They know what their stuff is worth." Indian Jewelry and Genuine Turquoise, Est. 1956. Sabra Shop (dates, figs, candy). Big Fella, Tall & Big. (Another shop services "Portly.") A drunk in hippy beads, embroidered denim, white shoes, stopped me near Tall & Big and said, "Hey, Charlie Parker died at thirty-eight and I'm forty-three and all I got to show is a Limo service...." Cute names: Oliver's Twist, Men's Fashions. Eliza Dolittle Flowers. View-tiful Real Estate at Ben Blank Co. Nates, Mr. Corned Beef of Palm Springs. Fun in the Sun Candy. Alive and Well in Palm Springs, A Plant Shop."

Of course, there are also Magnin's, J. and I., and Saks, and W & J Sloane, and Bullock's . . . "Shirts and Shoes Required."

Meanwhile, in the Sinatra compound, Frank, with his latest bride, Barbara Marx . . . who knows what charming mischief they are performing? According to Barbara, "He's turned every single day into Christmas." They are an inspiration to Palm Springs. The family that unwraps packages together stays together.

Palm Springs is in the business of intelligently engineering itself as a resort. A broad understanding of history, safaris, and the trots is not the local excitement. Shots are not required. You won't need a kit of medicines from your doctor. Both English and Beverly Hills are spoken. The Research Department of the Convention & Visitors Bureau, Michael E. Fife, Director, has done a series of studies for the use of persons in the recreation trade. "The average length of stay for all respondents remained 3.9 nights," he writes. A table tells us that the percentage of visitors from Missouri declined from .6 percent in 1971 to .4 percent in 1973. (Ohio gained a lot of Palm Springs contact during the same period. What's the matter, Missouri?)

Mr. Fife's little book entitled *Analysis of the High Income Hotel Visitor* tells us that Sun & Swimming is a runaway first among the types of recreation enjoyed, followed by Shopping, Sightseeing, Night Clubs, Golf, Therapeutic Facility (do they mean Melvyn's?), Visiting Friends and Relatives, Tennis, Horseback Riding, and Other. It's that Other that really interests me. 9.6 percent did a lot of Other in Palm Springs. Where do we meet, Nine Point Six Percent? What the people like is Climate, Atmosphere, Recreation, Relaxation, Topography, Restaurants, Shopping, Friendly People, No Pollutants and a few admit they like Other, too. Is the Other of "Like Most" the same Other of "What type of Recreation"? There is a dark side, too, which Mr. Fife's report does not scant. "What did you like least about Palm Springs?" Multiple responses were permitted. "Too many people," "expense," and "sand and wind" were at the head of this sad line, with "boring," "heat," and oddly enough, "pollution," up there too. My favorite "like least" was "hippies" (2.6 percent). Personally, I only saw one hippie, a gray-bearded middle-aged novelist, whom I met constantly when I brushed my teeth and karma or asked midnight questions about the meaning of life in my bathroom mirror at the Ingleside Inn.

Under "like least," there was a large number of "No Answers"—the tightlipped 32.7 percent. Having spent all that money, they ain't complaining. Their karma is quiescent.

Some of the small-town coziness of Palm Springs may have slipped away, but people still point out Alan Ladd's hardware store or the place where the electric golf cart first saw the light of day. The desert is dramatic and silent, only a few minutes from the Eldorado Club, where there is golf and the lockers clang and the private bottles chink.

For those who believe that heaven is not to be found in heaven, but rather, must be made on earth, Palm Springs, California, U.S.A., may be proof positive that they are on the right track. It is a very nice place to spend eternity. All you need is a little lotion for the skin dryness and some sport clothes. In Palm Springs's present mellow state—it no longer aspires to be Palm Beach—you don't even need sport clothes. You can wear jeans. You can wear your city shirt. You can just be who you please. You can even cut your own hair and ride a bicycle, if you're a famous movie star. You can do these things and dream you're a famous movie star, retired politician, distinguished foreign gentleman.

The Springs, "A Classic in Desert Living, the Fairway at Your Door, The Mountains Beyond," advertises "an advanced computer security system behind the guarded gates." Our fellow man is cowering in his gracious condominiums across from The Eisenhower Medical Center on Bob Hope Drive. Oh, this is strange. I remember when a simple, sweet, very much movie writer invited me down for a weekend and he said, "Wal, it's jes' a village, sonny. It's jes' folks hangin' out in the desert, a-eatin' of the health foods." Another new addition is the Desert Dawn Memorial Park, a mortuary and cemetery for those who want to be buried at Golf Club Drive.

An idea of news priority can be worked out through close

analysis of the first letter to the editor in an issue of *Palm Springs Life*, which complains that the magazine printed lots of pictures of Frank Sinatra, news, fashion, social, and advertising, but failed to put Ol' Blue Eyes on the cover when he committed matrimony with Barbara Marx. "Some of us could never get too much of what's happening with our favorite entertainer," says the writer, who points out that she is "not just a silly lady 'fan.' "

High Culture has also invaded the former village. An open letter from James E. Brown, Inc., "The General Contracting Firm Who Cares," appeals to Palm Springs to support The Center Theater—live people moving around on stage and saying word, word, phrase, phrase, back and forth. In recent years a new Library Center, new Desert Museum, and the new Center Theater for the Performing Arts have found generous patrons. The SunLiner city transit system had a little problem—bankruptcy—but still moves around town with its modern buses filled with decorator colors and background music.

An older attraction, the spectacular Aerial Tramway, which has served about four million people with high altitude thrills, continues its soaring pleasures, and has added cans of Fresh Mountain Pure Air and Bavarian Beer Fests for group ascensions. High-protein dinners, prime ribs and steak barbecues, nourish those tourists tuckered out by the ride and the challenging 360° views which extend as far south as Mexico. At appropriate times of the year, the Aerial Tramway sponsors dogsled races, Winter Photo Day, the Easter Sunrise Program, the Miss Tramway Beauty Pageant, and a New Year's Eve party which may be the highest event of its type. Four million visitors ago, I was one of the first to try out its inspiring views of desert and mountains, the abrupt change of temperature—maybe forty degrees—from start to finish, the technical marvel of stringing this ride into the sky.

One of the outstanding unnatural acts which civilization has performed with the desert is the swimming pools—nearly fifty-five hundred of them, or one for every two or three registered voters—so that they have changed the climate, creating cloud formations and rain bursts (desert exaggeration, pardner). There are also two-hundred and forty tennis courts in the area. The man-made Lake Cahuilla and the Salton Sea, marinas and yacht clubs, make this the wettest desert in memory—fishing, sailing, swimming in a territory once thought fit for camels. The imported camels have disappeared, although occasionally a desert rat with irrigated liver claims to see a last survivor. Burros are still used in steep mountain agriculture.

My own favorites among the major attractions are . . . But first I have to admit I used a bicycle more than a car, and spent the sunny winter mornings exploring the byways on a ten-speed. Okay, here are a few un-food, un-drink, un-tennis, un-golf, un-starlet pleasures, in case you want to break out of the beaten path:

Moorten's Desert Botanical Gardens displays two thousand varieties of desert flora. Indian lore, crystal, rock and wood miracles add to the educational browsing. Live birds and wildlife abound. I looked for Candy Bergen, who happened to be elsewhere. I saw an armadillo, however, and Mrs. Moorten speaking fluent botany.

The Living Desert Reserve, 360 acres, has a palm oasis, bird displays, trails. It reminds us of what was and still is, with a little initiative on the part of the tourist.

The Desert Museum also displays the natural history of the desert, and a collection of fine art, and primitive, California, and folk art, for those who hunger for such. I do. Sunday afternoon concerts make a welcome distraction from poolside and tennis labors. The College of the Desert, the Desert Symphony, The Valley Players Guild, and the Center Theater all offer cultural respite from ultraviolet overdose.

In addition to the usual offbeat attractions, I'd like to suggest some off-offbeat ones: Cabot's Old Indian Pueblo Museum in Desert Hot Springs, a Hopi-style building, is a trading post for tourists, but was constructed by one man over twenty years and has the odd, quirky, personal feeling of a butcher house. Miss Cornelia White's House, built from railroad ties in 1894, contains old Bibles, old beds, early paintings, the first telephone in Palm Springs, and a sense of the sleepy village of not so long ago. There is an antique quaintness about "Donations Accepted." Thirty-two miles away stands Pioneer Town, a frontier village used in western movies. And the Indian canyons nearby provide loneliness, nature, pensive occasions, animal and vegetable life, hiking, metaphysical inspiration, rock formations. You can bring a pastrami sandwich from Nate's Deli and imagine you're eating hardtack.

The Indian canyons, silent slashes of an ancient civilization, make a startling contrast to the luxuries of Palm Springs. The Cahuilla Indians, ancestors of the Agua Caliente tribe which still owns these tribal homesites, planted rare palms, used the icy mountain springs for irrigation of crops, and bathed in the hot springs. In the Andreas Canyon, there are dense groves of alders, willows, sycamores, wild grape, mesquite, and the ghosts of somebody's ancestors wander under the palms. I wandered into—not too far into —a cave in Murray Canyon, where there is also a band of wild ponies who are probably descendants of Indian ponies. The Tahquitz Falls was used in the original film of *Lost Horizon* to give an image of purity, dramatic nature, crushing impenetrable meaning. Hiking or horsebacking into the canyons, uncrowded by tourists, you can tell yourself you are one of the first after the Native Americans.

The Desert Museum deserves more than passing mention. Being new, the names of its donors—Disney, Sinatra, Annenberg—and the innovative architecture, combining volcanic stone, glass, outdoor sculpture gardens (there is, after all, no tradition for a great museum in the desert), have gained more publicity than the contents of the museum. Performing arts, libraries, education, and celebration of the community are part of the concept. And there is a small, growing collection of works of art, classic and modern paintings and sculpture. I happened on a traveling show of Rodin's *Burghers of Calais.* Implicitly, lots of money is also displayed, but the interesting and significant fact is that thousands of tourists and residents have already formed museum habits. They go, they stroll, they appreciate, they enjoy. It's not Florence or the Louvre yet. Some carry milk shakes in paper containers. But the sandbox players are coming of age, and the coming events in art, natural science, film, music, and wildlife are significant entrees to those for whom steak and brew, sun, golf, and tennis do not the whole person make.

This is a good place for idle hours. Puritan guilt doesn't feel guilty. Fun is the business around here, and the spending under the sun, in the healthful dry air, gives us an idea of what heaven might be like, if God could only afford it.

I didn't have the time to do everything I wanted to do. That's a big change from the old Palm Springs, where what you did was Nothing, Elegantly, day seamlessly following day.

Thank you, Ingleside Inn, for the loan of the bicycle and plenty of hot air to fill the tires. I played one last set of tennis with a man who happened to know both Kirk Kerkorian and Ol' Blue Eyes. He has a hustler's backhand. "Okay, Herb," he said, "wanna try another set for a taco and a milk shake?"

"Wal," says I, "gotta move on, across the pass where the sky meet the hills and the purple sage matches the hair of the Air California stew."

"Rot on. Ah hear yew, good buddy. Maybe yew better git one a them new metal Prince rackets so you kin cover the court. Bah now."

I rode my bike one last time out into the desert twilight, dusty, alone, in search of the meeting of temporal existence and external standards, hair cut and blown like your average eccentric desert tycoon's, and I wondered how I'd look as a ... nah! ... but maybe ... well, why not? ... as a prime time adventure series. Would Frankie or Kirk like to finance the pilot?

Such is the madness of life in the sun. Palm Springs, once a village for idle dreamers, is now a town which encourages active fantasies about pleasure, luxury, and glory. I didn't become rich and famous like everyone else, but I got some new muscles and a glimpse of another, tanner life-style. Perhaps this is enough for one week in the desert. If I'm not destined to be the star of a series entitled "Bikester of the Desert Empire," at least I can play Distinguished Foreign Gentleman in the pool of the Ingleside Inn at midnight.

5
Whatever Happened to Big Sur?

"Are you making a turn?" I sarcastically inquired of the gentleman blocking traffic at the corner in Carmel. His left arm was extended softly.

"No, I'm drying my nail polish," he said.

He was about sixty years old, with white hair, ruddy cheeks, a red L.L. Bean flannel shirt. He was driving a matching red Morgan without the belt around the hood. The good life in Carmel is tolerant, and this community is to Ye Olde Retirementland Village as St. Tropez is to Atlantic City. Aging, its best elegance behind it, but still swinging. A matronly fireman can find a loyal friend in the Navy officer with an astonishingly clean record, Bermuda shorts and a new, daring handlebar mustache. It tickles. Ladies who hid in closets for thirty-five years can finally come out freely in Carmel and stroll down Cinderella Lane, and enjoy the cheesecake (spelled *creeeamy* cheesecake) at the Thunderbird Bookshop/Restaurant, which purveys books, Japanese folk art, antiques and complete dinners with "melt-in-your-mouth popovers." It trusts its customers not to smear the creeeamy cheesecake on the stock of fifty thousand books, and to return them to the shelves after dining. It trusts them to buy a few sometimes. No other bookshop/restaurant can make this claim.

A younger crowd goes to swinging Monterey. A still younger crowd burrows into the secret valleys and crags, cliffs and canyons, slopes and beaches of stormy Big Sur.

The highway to Big Sur was opened in 1937, but the visitor has a sense of discovering a new place on the edge of the earth. California's Route 1 winds along sea and surf, hippie and mountain person, cloud and cypress, pine and yucca—the cypresses bleached white as bone, "fleeing before the wind," in Robert Louis Stevenson's phrase—to a community of some seven hundred inhabitants. Big Sur, a mountainous, cliffy redoubt on the Pacific, marked "Wild Area" on many maps, used to be famous for nothing but its beauty. Then, a generation ago, Henry Miller and Robinson Jeffers spent years in these environs, drawing other bohemians with them: poets, painters, wine lovers, who lived with the occasional intrusion of wild boar, mud slides, and neighborly nosiness from the nearby communities of Carmel (earthquake retreat from San Francisco) and Monterey (fishing metropolis gone in the direction of quaint and honky-tonk).

The wild boar in the Santa Lucia mountains, which sometimes have disturbed my campground, are a powerful breed, part Ukrainian and part native American porker. They can weigh 250 pounds—active pigment. When they come trampling among your sleeping bags, they can make you long for the Del Monte Hyatt House in Monterey. I tend, when camping out, to sleep lightly.

In the sixties, Big Sur became the world capital of what is called the Growth Movement. Esalen Institute, its workshops and life-style, occupied the magic hot springs that cured the Esselen Indians of what ailed them. (The Indians no longer exist.) And inland from the sea, in the forest, the Tassajara Zen Center was established—the largest Zen training center outside Japan, with monks from Texas and Harvard, lady monks, boy monks, and even some Oriental monks, now under the leadership of the Roshi Richard Baker, who succeeded the late Roshi Suzuki. They have guest cabins and hot sulfur springs and a swimming pool, too. My favorite route in is to hike from Arroyo Seco through the Los Padres National Forest, avoiding poison oak and wild boar wherever possible. I've usually succeeded with the latter, failed with the former. Once I took the road in which defeated the entire undercarriage of a Jaguar 3.8 I had rashly purchased on the recommendation of a movie producer (it would give me a bit of class, he said). I left the Jag with the monks, who planned to repair it in their Zen Jaguar Repair Shed and use it for carrying the Roshi Suzuki, but later decided to trade it in for a Ford pickup. They know the meaning of true inner peace and a trouble-free transmission. I may be the only middle-aged Jewish novelist from Cleveland, Ohio, ever to contribute a Jaguar to the Zen Buddhist order.

The morning bells sound. Chime, chime. The food is organic, tasty, loving. If there are flies in the dining room, the tonsured monks chase them out by flapping towels. A few years ago, one of the monks was a young woman who had been a creative writing student of mine at Harvard. This is not the Zen monastery of your dreams. Guests at the Tassajara Zen Center should reserve in advance. I have hiked in with children, wife and once with Big Bill Graham, the rock promoter, who took a vow of silence before we set out. The vow lasted ten minutes, when he began to say "Ouch" on the trail. He had bought his hiking boots the night before and broken them in by walking back and forth in front of the evening news on television. Walter Cronkite sometimes talks long, but not long enough.

Tassajara—which means "place-where-meat-in-strips-is-cut-and-hung-to-dry"—was a popular year-round resort among the now extinct local Indians. The seventeen hot mineral springs, sulfur, sodium, magnesia, iron, phosphate, steaming with that mysterious inner-earth volcanic heat, attracted Chinese coolie labor over a hundred years ago, and then stagecoach revelers, and then me hiking in from Arroyo Seco during the early sixties, and now the tranquil, boiling students of Zen Buddhism. Make reservations for the forest primeval. There is no pressure to believe or do anything. Be with someone you love, or with yourself. Bill Graham might be a good choice. Four A.M. chanting and seven-tone bells might be a change from room service at the Del Monte Hyatt House in Monterey.

A few hippies, troglodytes, and druids still survive in the valleys and caves near Big Sur, mountain people with ponytails and a wary independence, using words like "space" to describe something within rather than outside. For visitors, there are some famous facilities. Nepenthe, a restaurant and a way of life—fire, good drink, souvenir shop—began as a house built (it is said) for Orson Welles and Rita Hayworth. Then it was a family-run enterprise, early in the semidetached natural food field, with hollow-eyed, long-haired waitresses. Now it is an institution, with some of an institution's blandness of feeling despite the spectacular decor of the whole universe—cliffs, clouds, fogs and sea—surrounding it. A few men in ponytails, using words like "vibes," still come for the calories and to brood by the fire.

I brooded by the fire, bent against the evening chill. "Hey man," said one of the dropout mustaches. "Like me to crack your back?"

"What?"

"I'm a homegrown chiropractor, man. A Capricorn. Like me to give your back a crack?"

Whatever happened to Big Sur is still happening to it. Along with the boars, the condors, the mountain lions and the whales, the battered blue VW and the flower-painted camper are not yet extinct. A few mescaline nomads, peaceful and questing, sit on the beach in the lotus positions of their choice. History rolls off their backs like the morning fogs off the ridges.

In the old days, Nepenthe, by bend of sky and lurch of sea, off Route 1 there, was the center of "downtown Big Sur." (No mayor, no city hall, no real downtown, seven hundred souls if you don't count woodchucks and wild boar.) Nepenthe offered decent food, redwood accoutrements, glorious glassy promontories, outdoor fires, strong drink for them as liked strong drink. The family that took it over from Orson Welles and developed a restaurant (primary meaning: place where one restores the body and soul) still owns it. There is also now the Phoenix Shop; souvenirs, alas, but if you're a stranger, wal, you might need a guidebook or a primitive Taiwan set of matchbooks or a Japanese tatami mat for your prayers. There is authentic local jade. There is nearly authentic Indian jewelry.

Bob Overholt, the flaxen-haired maître d'hôtel at Nepenthe, with his long, flowing blond beard—what the San Francisco psychiatrist Francis Rigney calls the Passive Prophet Beard—turns out to be a dropped-out L.A. cop. Friendly. Nice. He described the new mood at Big Sur: fewer dropped-out hippies living in caves, little dope, only two kindly, compassionate policemen patrolling the roads. It is becoming a family resort. Lots of campers and trailers and recreational vehicles in the parking lots of Nepenthe. He recommended we visit Ventana, the elegant new hotel-restaurant up the road a piece. "Of course, I'm a chowhound, I loved G.I. food for four years, but still they got a great avocado and sour cream omelet, I think it is." He paused romantically. "All the waiters wear towels around their wrists. It's really stylish."

At the Nepenthe bar the conversation is not yet exactly Middle American. A bearded young man spoke of the bartender: "Once I shook his hand and I could feel he was a man of power."

"Really," said the radiant, relevant girl.

"He said he was happy to be in this space with us."

"Really," said the lady.

This may be a place where vocabulary is simplified, and Really means Yes, I do, I understand, I will, and Hello. But it is also a place where the sun shines, the fog rolls, the sea gleams, the hot springs beneath the surface bubble up, and the body takes pleasure in a museum of miraculous beauty. Really. "Space mates" tend to replace spouses among the residents, and there is never a fight, although sometimes an interpersonal conflict will break out. There is no window-shopping in this world-famous metropolis of seven hundred souls, but the general store or two can replace your sweat socks if you're a clothing buff. The little couturier around the corner is the Salvation Army Thrift Shop in Seaside. Somehow, the meditators at Ventana, the new luxury resort, are wearing Gucci loafers and Pierre Cardin shoulder bags over their jeans jackets, like characters out of *Flaming Gurus,* an underground movie never made. "The young people have a new and constructive attitude around here," said Bob, the maître d' at Nepenthe. "But you still have folks passing through for a month or two. Somehow it all works out. About an even number of men and women"—stroking his pale, squeaky-clean prophet's beard. "You just don't get those Hell's Angels giving a lot of lip. Those cycles. The two cops work as firemen, too; they do a lot of community service. We're pretty close. Campers. Trailers. Sociable around here is how I'd put it."

"What about the old hippies from the sixties? You were here during the time of the Herd of Independent Minds?"

"Yeah, I was getting divorced around then. There's still lots of artists and writers living around Big Sur. Partington Ridge, places like that. I know 'em all. That novelist, Jack what's-his-name, I see him a lot. I think he's still here. The mud slide a few years ago put us on the map again. Hell, we got national teevee coverage, three networks photographing how two buildings got a little smudged," said the laid-back veteran cop, tired of freeway hassles, now joining his love of candlelight romance and food with a second career in calorie management. "Yeah, people come and work our kitchen awhile, then they go to Deetjen's or Ventana or Fernwood, then they come back here. We got a tribal trip going. Mellowing out gradually now. Don't see much dope. It's a whole different ball game. They got towels over the waiters' arms at Ventana. I really like that style. Candles, the view, the sparkly air, a nice lady."

"How's the food over there?"

"Man, they got *towels on the arms.* The food has *got* to be good."

What was once the beatnik kingdom by the sea, which was also in due course the hippie kingdom in the mountains, the Big Sur of Henry Miller and Jack Kerouac, of the dropout druids and the runaway flower kids, buttons on their fronts and decals on their rears, love and confusion in their overflowing hearts, is now the new roughing-it resort. From San Francisco and Pasadena, San Diego and Denver, roll the campers with single parents and their charges; a daddy with a walkie-talkie cries, "Chuckie! Get me a Fresca! Roger and over!" among the towering pine, and the minuteman son in visored railway cap answers sweetly, "Roger and over, one Pepsi coming up."

There tends, at the entrance to parks, to be a sweet crunch of spent shells underfoot and the warble of the eight-track Fifth Dimension stereo version of *Hair*, a well-known musical of the last decade, which served to explain astrology to folks on the ground at Ticketron Central. Thoughtful families move more deeply into Pfeiffer-Big Sur State Park, Point Lobos, John Little State Reserve, and they visit the Old Gold Mines, Pfeiffer Beach (Pacific Ocean endless out there, sea lions barking and whales spouting), the agitated streams that hurtle through the Santa Lucia Range, the twisting canyons that are still silent and inviting of adventure.

My automobile startled three baby deer on the road. I stopped short, but one ran straight for my fender, grazed it, leaped across the road and over the fence, rump twitching reproachfully. I did my best, little Bambi. The thump was little more than a kiss. The wilderness at Big Sur is still merely kissing urban amenity, and is comfortable for nature. Bring calamine lotion.

Though the Big Sur Construction & Supply Company pickup wore a bumper sticker on its own reproachful rump: SIERRA CLUB GET LOST.

In the old days, Deetjen's Big Sur Inn—a rustic European family hostel, built snugly against the hillside, run by a family with family feeling, books in every room, tasty food—used to be the hideout-getaway for artists and writers from San Francisco and Los Angeles. The proprietor, Helmuth Deetjen, had his eccentricities, and many times I stayed there, gossiping about the history of Big Sur—"land to the south," he called it. The beds were not the most comfortable; sometimes you could hear highway noises from Route 1 or your neighbor's night sounds; but the redwood and driftwood and shingles and spirit of the place compensated for what it lacked in corporate hotel management skill. Mr. Deetjen has passed to the land above. Now, alas, the place is still eccentric, but the old family feeling is gone; reservations are honored capriciously by a manager who says he spent time in an ashram and points out that he *irons* his Levi shirts. This manager, Ed Somebody, looked at me with burning eyes and informed me: "I remember you. You have burning eyes. Very distinctive. I notice such things." He then added that he had made a mistake with my reservation and was not honoring it. "I'm sorry," he said. "I can put you up in the shed if you don't find anything else." If he had been made of paper, my burning eyes would have ignited him on the spot. I saw a certain look of delight on his face. In the ashram a fella doesn't have a lot of power.

Well, I had a bad experience with my old hideaway, but it adds to the adventure of the road, not to be welcomed at the Inn, doesn't it? Ave, Helmuth Deetjen, your spirit still prowls the trails and beaches, looking for flotsam to add another room.

On to Ventana. Yes, they did wear those forearm towels, just as the veteran at Nepenthe promised they would. And the rooms at the Inn, of which an L.A. music tycoon is president, are expensive. But there are deer in the meadows and a certain amount of uneconomical care in the appointments, and the vistas are grand.

Nepenthe is no longer full of voluptuous women with peasant blouses that slide off the shoulder. But Bob says, when asked about love and what a bachelor like himself does for love: "Well, people pass through. Sometimes they stay for a month or two, or five years sometimes. But the old families never accept you."

Our hamburger at Nepenthe cost a lot. It was a good hamburger.

Our sand dabs at Ventana cost more and other things added to the bill. But they were good sand dabs, good other things.

The view follows you, free, wherever you go.

At the Esalen sign just off Route 1, south of Nepenthe, at the little hill and road on which the sixties found their innocence in the form of the Human Potential Movement, the old shop is still in good repair, despite its retreat from publicity. The media butcher shop chopped Esalen into hamburger, but like Prometheus, it still exists, chained to its rock of self-fulfillment, liver exposed to the vultures. I visited during a crowded weekend of workshops and demonstrations, including a Zen sword master who sliced, blindfolded, an apple placed on the uncovered navel of his assistant (a whoosh through the air, stopping just short of disembowelment, and a burst of applause as the neatly split apple tumbled off the belly). What's the Japanese word for William Tell? And Gabrielle Roth, a long and lissome dark creature, who looks like the lovely, drowned Radcliffe lady in an evil *New Yorker* cartoon, was conducting her class in Movement. She moved magnificently. Her students in the Huxley room moved less magnificently. She sang a little improvised couplet about appreciating their divine bodies as they swayed and undulated. Their bodies were mostly not divine, but they sang and swayed and undulated and seemed on the road to being convinced. Her voice was deep and rich. She said she is not "into publicity," but perhaps there is a place in the guru field for a handsome young photogenic woman like Gabrielle. I suspect some videotape person—"into videotape"—will introduce her to the larger world. There will always be a market for a beautiful young woman who can bring divinity to those afflicted with cellulite and self-doubt.

Then I headed down the slope to the baths. Incense, candlelight, crashing surf, natural sulfur springs. There is nothing to equal them for sensual, not necessarily sexual, delight. The water urges you to be quiet, to be talkative, to be yourself at peace. The dark spirit of the Esselen Indians broods over us, as someone's "space mate"—intimate, not necessarily sexual, partner—informed me. The air was fresh. I boiled, steamed, and contemplated the whales and sea lions below, to the west, in the turbulent surf. Grooviness, framed by natural loveliness, is alive and well.

Point Lobos—Wolf Point—is named for what the Spanish called "sea wolves" and we call sea lions, swimming in packs, herding, sometimes barking their odd, deep, sharp call. You can hear it on the narrow beaches and wild rocks when you stop and climb down to the shore. Starfish, abalone, purple anemones, marine animals of all sorts grow like the flowers that once covered the state of California, so that you can hardly step without trampling a dozen blossoms. The ridges of the Santa Lucia mountains begin almost at the sea, with fir, creamy-blooming yucca plants, and memories of the days when Robert Louis Stevenson camped nearby, a hundred years ago. The Big Sur River is a mild stream for its name, but all the other facts of nature are grand here. It is not country for sunning and idle loafing. Visitors have to make their own nests and amusements, outside of a few hotels. "Downtown Big Sur" boasts no movie house, concert hall, or city amenity, other than a post office, recently obliterated by a winter mud slide. Satisfactions are of nature, and particularly of one's own nature—inner.

My bad luck forced me to leave Big Sur. I packed up my sweat socks and blue denim and climbed into my VW—on which the juice of fir had dripped—and headed north toward normal life, Carmel, Monterey, and home in San Francisco.

Carmel has sidewalks now. It didn't used to. It has shopping centers. It has retired teachers and officers and art lovers and unisexual couples who have successfully raised and sent out into the world their ecological quota of well-brought-up poodles. The Hansel-and-Gretel houses, the sugarplum cottages, the redwood doodle-maisons still give a doll-like charm to this city. Joan Baez, who used to live nearby with her peace institute, has taken her guitar and her racy Jaguar elsewhere, up the road a piece toward San Francisco.

I stopped for a sweet and tasty Sunday brunch in the Swedish Restaurant, which is run by Danes (the cook is French and Jewish). The Swedish-French-Danish-Jewish pancakes were delicious with somethingberry jam. Martyrs to Sunday brunch stood lined up in an autumn drizzle under gold umbrellas, awaiting their turn on the street outside. The lines were even longer at the Tuck Box down the street.

The Poetic Art of Name Your Restaurant has been carried to refined heights in Carmel. The Bully III, the Esperanto, the French Poodle, the Highway Robbery, the Hog's Breath (owned by Clint Eastwood, it is said), Peyton's Place, the Piscean, the Shabu-Shabu (four-seventeenths of a haiku) give some of the flavor of verbal dining. Monterey's Cannery Row, Carmel Valley, Monterey Fisherman's Wharf, Pacific Grove, Pebble Beach, Seaside—the adjacent communities—share in the pleasure of cute retirement living and resort street-strolling. The Spanish missions and monasteries, the remnants of sardine fishing in Steinbeck country (now old-towned over by development), the festivals (Bach, pop, jazz, antique car, Townsend Plan), the many little theaters and galleries, all will tend to keep you away from your teevee. There are palmists if you need help reading your hand. There are astrologers for those who want to know if tax-exempt city bonds can be trusted.

A graffito in a Monterey Fisherman's Wharf john tells

something of the enduring philosophic mood of Big Sur, Carmel, and the Monterey Peninsula, which could be called Laid-Back California Existentialism. *The answer is not Sex. That is the Question. The answer is Yes.*

The ruddy, white-haired man blocking traffic with the drying nails of his left hand extended in Carmel was right, and I was wrong. He had decompressed from the Twentieth-Century Hustle. I need to spend more time on Route 1, rambling along the trails of Big Sur.

III
Lonely Ones, Making Out

A FEW EXCERPTS FROM BILL GRAHAM'S REVIEWS

"Bill Graham's Fillmore East, the undisputed Mecca of rock audiences and rock musicians . . ."—*Wall Street Journal*

"Bill Graham's arms swirl through the air like boomerangs, each one returning clutching a phone . . . He looks at the silver watch on his right wrist that has two faces giving Eastern and Western time, and launches into another tirade on what seems to be four phones at once. 'The man is insane,' he yells to the ceiling, 'and he doesn't wash under the arms.'"—*The Financial Times* (London)

"In a world where indolence, inefficiency, and fiscal fecklessness are the rule, Graham is a nonpareil. He has grown rich by knowing what is good, and hiring the best talent he can get. He provides his performers with the best equipment and facilities, and expects them to be good. . . ."
—*Time*

"Rip-off artist! Pig! Rip-off artist."
—Street cries.

"A genius of a producer . . . an abrasive, complex personality . . . an orphan . . . During the Korean conflict he was court-martialed for insubordination, but was discharged with the Bronze Star . . ."
—*Cue*

"'They even provide us free beer,' said Country Funk's guitarist . . ."
—*Newsweek*

"'If you're a bank robber, it doesn't mean much if you knock over a bank at Elephant's Tusk, Missouri,' Graham said. 'If you're big time, you aim for a Times Square bank at noon, right?'"
—*The Washington Post*

"Graham has also done dozens of benefits—benefits that really do benefit their causes, and for groups that wouldn't have a chance on the ordinary benefit circuit. . . . The gashlike lines between his

nose and chin add to the aura of ready menace. . . . 'If I have to choose between liking and respect, I'll take the latter.' "
—*The New York Times Magazine*

"With so many cities facing racial violence, we can hope that other Bill Grahams will come forward to take over the leadership in these troubled areas and win the respect of whites and Negroes alike. The need is great, the time is short."—The Hon. Thomas M. Rees, in "The Graham Crusade," a tribute and history inserted in The Congressional Record. The Representative may have confused Bill Graham with Billy Graham.

6
A Zen Hike with Bill Graham

"A roshi is a person who has actualized that perfect freedom which is the potentiality for all human beings. He exists freely in the fullness of his whole being. The flow of his consciousness is not the fixed repetitive patterns of our usual self-centered consciousness, but rather arrives spontaneously and naturally from the actual circumstances of the present. The results of this in terms of the quality of his life are extraordinary—buoyancy, vigor, straightforwardness, simplicity, humility—"

(Well, I'll have to strike that 'simplicity' and 'humility' for Bill Graham.)

"—serenity—"

(That one, too.)

"—joyousness, uncanny perspicacity, and unfathomable compassion. His whole being testifies to what it means to live in the reality of the present. Without anything said or done, just the impact of meeting a personality so developed can be enough to change another's whole life. . . . The Extraordinariness we see is only our own true nature . . . a deep flow of being and joy in the unfolding of Buddha mind."

These words, cited by the roshi Richard Baker about the roshi Shunryu Suzuki, of the Zen Mountain Center of Tassajara, California, also apply to Bill Graham, the monster promoter-in-chief of American rock music, proprietor of the Fillmores East and West and of the various Fillmore enterprises, with a few other modifications not usual to advanced roshiness: Bill has made millions of dollars, yells a lot, and now has sore feet. His improvisational language forced an "R" rating on the movie *Fillmore* (in this case, "R" does not stand for Roshi). He is a master of the put-down and the shut-up. He is one of the great telephoners of our time. He has won the Sitting Indoor Desk-Pounding & Telephone Screaming Contest every year since he started competing, and how he has won is with energy, wit, logic, and naked verbal maximum abusive charisma. He knows that the race is to the quick and the heavy; he is a quick and he is a heavy. He also knows how to honor.

How he got the sore feet: I had a vision of hiking with Bill Graham from Arroyo Seco, in the Las Padres Forest, into the Zen Mountain Center, bringing together two California marvels, man and institution. No telephones, no offices, vow of silence optional. I said to him: "It'll be a pleasure." He had nine thousand things to do, by actual count, including the opening of his movie and a Rolling Stones Tour of the United States. His staff pleaded: "Bill, you can't leave us now." His executive assistant called to say: "I'll tell you what, we'll fly you to New York, our expense, you can follow Bill on his rounds, have a lot of fun, get a great story, meet the superstars."

I said: "My heart is set on a Zen hike."

There was a moment of silence. The silence was saying: "What, you'd rather eat peanut butter sandwiches with some shaved-headed freaks than cavort in Manhattan with some long-haired freaks?"

Although I often use words, I know that silence has power. I clung to the gift of silence with both hands.

He said: "Bill can't make it. Nine thousand things to do—"

I said: "Okay, that's all right, I understand. Money and power come first—" (Oh, the gift of sarcasm and hurtie feelings.)

"He'll call you back," his assistant said.

Bill called back: "I'll pick you up on the morning. I'm buying my boots and pack now."

He telephoned once more with a threat: "We're gonna walk into the Zen woods with our vow of silence, my boots, my pack on my back, and in the middle of the forest I'm gonna unzip my pack and up will shoot an aerial and out will come my port-o-phone and I'll start doing business with both coasts. Schmuck."

Oh Lord, won't you buy me a Mercedes-Benz? I thought of his friend Janis Joplin as we got into the successor to Bill's MG, a Jaguar XKE, top down. He hadn't worn his hiking boots before we set out. His feet started to hurt even as we drove south from San Francisco and through the Carmel Valley toward the Las Padres Forest. Foreboding. But I remembered Shunryu Suzuki's description of Zen Mind: "It is wisdom which is seeking for wisdom."

It would have been wise to suggest to Bill that he break in his boots first, or ask his boot assistant to break them in. In the sutra it says, "There are no eyes, no ears, no nose, no tongue, no body or mind . . ." But did the Buddha ever try hiking ten miles across forest, mountain, and streams with stiff new boots? There are feet, Buddha. There is evil in the world, however the wisdom of the East slices it, and in this case, alas, I represented the sin of omission. O Brothers, would *you* have remembered to say: "Bill, listen. So wear the boots a few hours a day for two weeks ahead of time, while you're telephoning the Stones, cursing out Santana, dealing with the police and the presidents of record companies, firing secretaries, hiring assistants, bailing out musicians, entertaining your son, managing your divorce, promoting your film (*Fillmore,* a rock documentary about the closing of the Fillmore, starring Bill Graham), running benefits for the marijuana initiative and free clinics and any other good cause that corners you in a weak moment, brawling with Hell's Angels, cajoling international superstars, and in general, making a new life somewhat similar to your old one?"

I forgot. He put on the shoes that fateful Sunday morning, after one last transatlantic call to Mick Jagger, and off we roared, stopping only for barbecued steaks in Soledad, California, in a beer-and-grill that looked like the place where the families of death-row convicts gather for a moment of communing with scotch, sirloin, and humming fluorescence.

On to the dark and trackless forest.

Bill's Jaguar XKE down dirt and rutted roads to Arroyo Seco, near a diminishing late spring stream and the horsebridge named Horsebridge. We parked. We slipped on our packs. His feet hurt already. We began hiking in the direction of mountain, river, poison oak, unmarked paths which lead to the Zen monastery hidden deep in the forest. The first three experienced hikers of whom we asked directions each gave us a different fork in the trail. The trail was not marked on our map. It seemed as if we were setting out in all three directions. The monks don't need visitors to rip off their peace, and they have planted roaring waters, earth convulsions, and dangerous herbs in the way. *"What is this?"* Bill asked. "I should be on the phone to the Stones. I should be on a talk show in New York."

"Pleasure comes first. Think of this as pleasure," I said.

"I'm getting a blister."

"Remember, it's a pleasure."

We had either six or eleven miles to go, depending on which path we followed. But we didn't know which path we were following.

The Beatles sang that the sun had come, and the Beatles sang that it was all right, it was all right.

It would be sad to die in the forest for mere pleasure. But pleasure, as Bill Graham knows, means to be a winner. Now the task was to hike from mid-noplace to beautiful somewhere, trudging along with packs on back and sweat running down that mighty media-soaked head, and taking note of the fact that the world is a peculiar place. The orphan survivor from Berlin, the streetfighter from the Bronx, the Bronze-Star winner from Korea, the road-building paymaster and hustling character actor, the middle-aged revolutionary rock millionaire were now at one with a fellow whose shoes pinched. Desperation adrenalin spurted, despair muscles clinched, lymph filled the swellings in Bill's new $76.00 plus tax boots. Dear Pushpin Studios: Please design white space to stand for the Vow of Silence:

Which is filled with suffering unalloyed. When the silence is broken, Bill's undaunted face is blue with pain. We stop and lean against volcanic rocks decorated with dull-green, three-leaf vines. He removes his shoes. He will do the rest of the climb barefoot. No, I suggest, wear two pair of socks. Rocks, twigs, vines, brambles, burrs, bugs, and maybe six miles to go.

Okay, we'll talk. Bill reminisces. He was one of eleven Jewish children to survive a wartime hike from Berlin to Paris to Africa; two hundred started. He can't remember anything until he was ten, but his sister tells him he studied the violin from the age of five to nine. His name used to be Wolfgang Grajanka, and he wishes it still were. He learned to be a streetfighter as an adopted child in the Bronx. His ideal was John Garfield: tough, beetle-browed, a smoker, a destroyer of women. His beautiful secretary used to be Otto Preminger's beautiful secretary. If she could stand Preminger, she could surely bear Graham (in fact, like most people who hang out with him, she has fallen into loyalty and fervor, which is better than love for a businessman with a hundred-odd employees, several corporations, enough equipment to furnish the sound system of Purgatory). He started out with Bonnie, his ex-wife, a stapler, and a Vespa, putting up Fillmore posters for the first concert in the middle of the night. Oh yes, before that, as a businessman-actor for the San Francisco Mime Troupe, street guerilla pioneers, he had run a benefit which gave him, like, a little idea that something was happening among the kids out there. A few leaves fall from the calendar. Good God, some slick franchise operators are offering him a cool million and a quarter just for his name, and also the Fillmore name, and to open a chain of fifty-seven Fillmores. "All I'd have to do is cut the ribbons and put my papal Graham blessing on it in Cleveland, Denver, Jacksonville, Houston . . . Kosher! I'd be the psychedelic Joe Louis. I'd be Colonel Sanders." He shook his head. "Not for money. No portable Las Vegas, man."

His face was gray. I couldn't carry him, for sure. But he marched on like a psychedelic Sergeant Valley Forge in his bloody socks.

"Tell me more, Bill," I pleaded. I replaced the Vow of Silence with a Vow of Garrulity. As long as we were talking, he would move. It would soon be six o'clock. I thought I saw the caca of wild boar in the dim path. Nothing overhead but hawks, eyeball-eating vultures, and a few Air Force jets practicing to wipe out the enemies of democracy. The trail crossed the stream thirteen or fourteen times. Tension radiated into Bill's body through his tortured wads of feet. Here we were in Downtown Las Padres Forest, no telephones, only small animals, lizards, snakes, and trees, and he couldn't even relieve himself by clobbering me for getting him into this. He had stood up to maddened rock stars, record producers, cops, junkies, Hell's Angels, and now one mild-mannered novelist was causing him all this pain and he couldn't do the necessary: wipe him out. Well, we're friends.

A long zigzag trail up a steep face.

Pushpin Studios, please do another Vow of Silence. I walked ahead to persuade him there was no use stopping. Silence:

End of silence as we cheer ourselves into the monastery. We have done about six hours, nearly nonstop, with two adequate feet between the two of us. Spirits rise as Zen trainees offer us dinner, now being served in the organic dining room from which flies are customarily chased by flapped towels and monks herding them toward the open window. Haha, folks say when we tell of what roundabout trail we followed, how sore the toes, instep, soles. The food is organic, healthy, strong: breads, honeys, veggies, salads. Bill Graham, a celebrity among these monks, generously tells stories. We clap each other on the back. *Made it!*

The Tassajara Zen Mountain Center, gongs, clicks, sitting zazen, the whole smear, is the largest Zen training center outside of Japan, but it's not your ordinary Zen training center. A hundred years ago it was a mountain retreat; before that the Tassajara Indians enjoyed the magic hot springs. Isolated and pure, certain Zen fellow travelers, such as Bob Dylan and Allen Ginsberg, thought to buy the immense and lovely valley, under the auspices of Shunryu Suzuki:

"The sound of running water is his great speech—"

Now, with the death of Suzuki-roshi, the chief priest is Richard Baker-roshi, and the relationship between training monks and visitors in retreat is a sweet one, abetted by vegetarian meals, the swimming pool and the narrows of the stream, the hiking, the talk, and the thermal baths. Many of the monks are married; some are courting. There is much laughter. Although first-time visitors don't expect a lot of monks from Houston and the Lower East Side, they soon accept the pleasures of this odd vocation.

I had three cakes for dessert. Hungry after the day's walk.

Bill and I headed, he limping, for the hot baths. Dear Pushpin Studios: Not necessary to design ahs, ohs, groans of heterosexual male comradeship and pleasure in survival. Bill's blood circulated toward his feet. We lay and swam in the steaming tubs. "Well, it's all worth it, isn't it, Bill?"

"I wanted to hit myself," he said.

"Is that all?" I asked.

"You were walking too far ahead of me. I couldn't hit you," he said.

Next day we would consider purifying our souls by practicing meditation (sitting zazen), chanting sutras, eating in the Zendo, attending lectures, or perhaps just limping back through the forest. ("The color of mountains is Buddha's pure body.") Bill slept the sleep of the just and the suffering. I cranked up the one phone in the monastery to send a signal to the outside world. Good old Bill, he didn't even call his office or the Rolling Stones in London.

For our departure the sweet Zen monks of Tassajara gave us a lunch of health and organic—dates, figs, honest crunchy peanut butter on honest crunchy Zen bread, fruit, non-grass brownies. Bill worried that these good things might ruin his health, since he ordinarily synthesizes chlorophyl and protein from a steady diet of hamburgers and teevee dinners (sometimes he keeps his metabolism going by heating up three teevee foil trays at 2:00 A.M.).

Roshi Dick Baker gave us the V salute (that's V for Vegetarian) as we departed. Half the V for Vegetarian salute is Bill Graham's famous greeting. It only uses one finger, the central and longest one.

Back to Bill's XKE, parked at Horsebridge, and then on down the road to Route 101 and a return to business in San Francisco. We talked about the Rolling Stones' tour of gratitude which culminated in Altamont. "Gratitude? That'd be like I put on a gold lamé suit, hired a plane, and dropped one live chicken on starving Biafra." He was driving in his stocking feet. Melissa Dilworth, the rock critic and hiking expert, had telephoned her advice to keep his feet out of the sun so the flies don't get them. "I hiked through f—ing Pebbleland," he snarled. "I enjoyed my misery so much I didn't even write on my three-by-five cards."

We stopped for donuts and coffee, necessary to save Bill's life after the Zen health menace-food. "Winchell's Donuts are America's Favorites." The millionaire rock producer had to pay three cents extra for a cup of water on Route 101 at Winchell's Donuts. A sign read: "WE ARE PLEASED TO ANNOUNCE THAT THERE HAS BEEN NO INCREASE IN OUR PRICES SINCE THE ESTABLISHMENT OF THE WAGE & PRICE FREEZE. WINCHELL'S DONUTS, 'AMERICA'S FAVORITES.' "

The waitress kept a good eye on us. Her pink plastic curlers were set to go off if we made one false move. We looked like desperate characters, scarfing up America's favorites. Bill's normal tailor is the freaks who left their hats, coats, scarves at the Fillmore. "I send them to Meader's Cleaners first." It's not that he doesn't like his own clothes; he's very tight with his eleven-year-old Mime Troupe corduroy pants and his two sweatshirts. His bounty with friends and performers, with causes and benefits, with his former wife and his son, doesn't extend to spending money on dressing himself. He has soul; he doesn't need to spend money on shirts. He spends money on donuts. He has none of the modern youth-shlock disease which could be called Illusions of Gender. He doesn't need to be surrounded by pretty girls, like James Aubrey or, say, Bernard Cornfeld. He seems to be secure in his masculinity—as secure as a violent and kindly Jewish neurotic Bronze-Star-winning war hero refugee can be imagined to be. He does enjoy wheels, however, his tradition of transportation, from the boyish Vespa to the mighty XKE in which we were now rolling again, top down, feet bare, across the leveled countryside of northern California. We knew we were near home when a rust-colored Continental containing two ladies with identical rust-colored Afro wigs drew alongside and began honking at us, indicating non-Zen delights at the nearest off-ramp.

"Let's come up here again with our women," he said.

Back in San Francisco, we stopped at his office—factory, printing facilities, electronic shop, interlocking sets of rooms and enterprises. Assistants and secretaries trailed after him, asking orders and receiving suggestions: "Throw him out. Say yes. I'll call back. Why not?" They usually trailed off with the question, "Say, Bill, you're not wearing shoes anymore?"

He left for New York the following day to help promote one of his projects. He uses the word f— a lot. He means it. He makes it work for him. He telephoned from New York, between talk shows, to ask what I thought of fighting the "R" rating on a movie. "They say the word f— is an obscenity, but you and I know it's just the shortest distance between two points."

I tried to explain that not everybody knows how essential

it is to the life of the streets, in which not everyone is raised. Some have forgotten. The movie-raters are trying to forget.

"Uh-huh, uh-huh," he said, "and by the way"—adding a lot of "R"- and even "X"-rated language—"what I really called to say, Herb, is I had a wonderful time on our pleasure trip and I GOT A F—ING CASE OF POISON OAK, YOU—"

O my brothers, the future is passing swiftly into the past, but Bill Graham has risen through the convulsions of youthquake into personality, a genius and joy beyond any successful promotion. He is ready for the present again, as he has always been, with a holler, a curse, the compassion of strength, and a bottle of Calamine lotion. Nietzsche said in *The Anti-Christ:* "It is only the powerful who know how to honor, it is their art, their domain for invention."

I had a plaque made, with the following inscription:

> ZEN TORTURE SORE FEET PLEASURE HIKE
> FIRST PRIZE BILL GRAHAM

and placed it on the belly of a newly-minted Chinese trophy-shop Buddha. I hope he keeps it with his million-selling gold records, his Fillmore posters, his print of Bill Graham playing Bill Graham in *Apocalypse Now,* and his memorabilia of a full life in the magic magnification of media.

I too have poison oak. I itch, burn, scratch, wouldn't have done without this little two-day stroll with Bill Graham-roshi.

7
A Twenty-Year Talk with William Saroyan

For twenty years now, I have been conducting a continuous conversation with William Saroyan in the form of short, widely spaced paragraphs. We first met at the San Francisco Museum of Art when I took notice of a burly, black-mustached Armenian gentleman doing the divorced-father dance with one son, one daughter, explaining the sense and nonsense of maze construction. The picture I had in mind was of the handsome, exotic boy writer of "The Darling Young Man on the Flying Trapeze," *My Name Is Aram, My Heart's in the Highlands,* the early stories, novels and plays of great success—the careless gambler from Fresno who bragged and laughed his way to New York. This was not the man I saw, this shy and hopeful swain wooing his own children. But I recognized him anyway: from the deep rise and resonance of voice, and from an aura of personage that was unmistakable.

We talked, and then occasionally met. He was dividing his life between Fresno—because the company of the Armenians there and the local melons were good—and Paris, with a few short visits a year to camp out with relatives in San Francisco. He was well into the process of disengagement from the literary scene. What he wrote about his life was public and high-styled. His life itself seemed to be increasingly inward and colored with melancholy. He had the gifted melancholic's ability to be a hilarious entertainer, riffing on life and literature with unflagging wonderment. He seemed lonely.

Once he consented to spend an evening with some young women. When he arrived to meet his date, shining and dapper, it was clear that he had checked her out in an instant and decided she was too young. With the miraculous efficiency of Zero Mostel changing before one's eyes into a rhinoceros, William Saroyan changed into an Uncle. We were no longer two couples heading for dinner; we were a tour group led by a benevolent country visitor, who showed us Turk Murphy's Dixieland Band at Earthquake McGoon's in North Beach, and lectured about the Bohemian San Francisco that was. The young woman might have preferred lascivious behavior; Saroyan chose to be courtly, and made sure it was so much fun that his fan would not be disappointed.

When he met my Chinese housecleaner, he recognized that she was part Hawaiian and discussed with her the history and legends of Hawaii. When we ate at the Brighton Express in North Beach, he enlisted waiter, owner, cook, and patrons in a discussion of who should speak with the voice of God in his new play; I believe God was to be a horse in this case. When Mark Schorer tried to engage him to lecture at the University of California at Berkeley, a complex dance ritual ensued: Saroyan said: "Yes"; Schorer said: "When?"; Saroyan said: "Oh, soon"; Schorer said: "We arc an institution, Bill, we have to schedule, we have to get the money." Saroyan said: "Tell you what, Mark. Suppose I'm in New York and planning to drive to San Francisco. Suppose then I get in my car and I send you a postcard from Nebraska that I'll be in California toward the beginning of the month or so . . ."

He liked the idea. He just didn't want to be pinned down.

Another time, just after the Six Day War, I passed through Paris with the woman I was about to marry and we spent an evening with him at a café table. He talked about how he lived—wine, cheese, a little place in Montmartre, doesn't see anyone; uses the newspaper as tablecloth, so he can conveniently eat and read at the same time, and then clean up in a jiffy. He was doing some writing that day—most days —and left early. I had felt we were imposing on his time, but in a book a few years later he evoked our visit with generous sweetness.

As the years went by, we met once in a while. He joked, he was bitter about publishers, lawyers, agents, and fashion, he laughed, he didn't care. He was mad about writing as always, but he was not so crazy about most of the people he was meeting in adult life. His marriage and divorce, twice, to and from the same woman, was not a happy memory. His tax troubles, his gambling, his fluctuations on the literary stock market, the eccentricities and conniving for attention in the arts, his children, his difficulties with producers. . . . He was no longer some kind of laughing lad from Fresno. The world had seared him a little.

He still wrote about children and old men, about funky Armenians and cheerful babblers, but he also wrote movingly and with great power and even a bit of malevolence about the troubles of American marriage, about the pains of fatherhood, about the astonishment of a young man who looks in a mirror and discovers an old one looking back at him. This is an undiscovered Saroyan, exploring the reality of his life at an age, his early seventies, when most of his contemporaries are either dead or spending their time on television talk shows.

We corresponded occasionally. When I sent him my books, he responded with an open heart, living through another writer's work with attention. He inscribed one of his own books, "May the next year be Okay. That's all we can really expect."

More and more he seemed to prefer his own company. A journalist who traveled to Fresno to interview him was turned away at his door. But this spring, when I found myself making a trip to Fresno with Ari, one of my twin sons, I telephoned Saroyan from the yogurt factory we were visiting. I expected reluctance to receive unexpected visitors. "Ari?" he said. "Is that a Greek or a Hebrew name? Why don't you come on over?"

I told Ari he was going to meet a wonderful writer, a great man, and we drove to the bland, flat middle of Fresno, where Saroyan has a modest house and a few fig trees. My son, aged eight, and Bill, aged seventy-one, discussed their problems as young writers. The house looked a little like an assiduous graduate student's pad: piled with manuscripts, books, magazines, filmy glasses and cups, tables bending under the weight of paper. Saroyan is a bit deaf and his stomach bothers him. But he hears well enough and speaks loudly enough for a deaf world and we drank strong tea through the afternoon. He marveled that some people die or kill themselves, that so many writers give up. He was mystified and pained by the suicide of Hemingway and of so many poets. "I'm growing old!" he shouted. "I'm falling apart! And it's VERY INTERESTING!"

He still loves show biz, crime biz, sport biz, drink biz, but is quite irritable about their near relations, such as media biz, the lawyers who represented his ex-wife, millionaire rock singers with women's names, the accumulated animadversions of an optimistic young man fighting the blues all his life. He is scarred. The sorrow is hectic with wit, but grief is also admitted through the filtration system. He is a character writer who has gone from Young Leading Man to Wounded Sage—a long, un-American survival trajectory through "discontent, depression, impatience, annoyance, anger, and despair." He is, in fact, even though he has found it necessary to tell us so, a joyous melancholic survivor.

In Paris he still lives in his Spartan digs, surrounded by the history of Montmartre. He frequents the markets; he sniffs in the streets (better fun, he says, since he has given up smoking), he is not very sociable, and he writes. In Fresno he lives in two small tract houses next door to each other, filled with accumulation—besides the papers, books, letters, manuscripts published and unpublished, there are bowls of grapes, figs, and other fruit from his two backyards, including walnuts from his two walnut trees, and an old bicycle, askew prints; none of it dirty or really messy. He is surrounded by the tools of his trade, by his history. The reason for the second house was the hope that his two children might want to see Fresno and stay a while; they don't. His Armenian cousins drop in to help out. He spoke of thousands of old 78s—songs, operas and symphonies—but we talked too much to take time to hear music. His work is writing, he says, "but my real work is being."

He let Ari touch the ancient Royal typewriter on which he works. For some reason he wanted us to write down the names of Ari and his brother and sister and the maiden name of my former wife. He wanted to meet Ari's brother, Ethan, and when he returned to San Francisco, Ari received a typescript of a story called "Gaston" signed, "For Ari Gold from his Friend William Saroyan Fresno February 17, 1979." The story begins:

"They were to eat peaches, as planned, after her nap, and now she sat across from the man who would have been a total stranger except that he was in fact her father."

The accompanying letter to me discussed the fact that we have known each other for many years ("such progressions are not without interest"); the metaphysical quality of the word *perhaps;* a visit he had made to a Veterans Hospital; also Blake, Nabokov, Gogol, Leon Edel, Henry James, and the nature of autobiography. He concluded by asking what he should read to know more about Haiti.

Ari and Ethan read the story, which they decided should be called "The Peach," and Ari said with the deepest and strongest voice he could muster: "It's VER-RY INTEREST-ING!"

When they don't use themselves up, America tends to use up its writers, and when I gave a young friend some stories of Saroyan's to read, she loved them and asked, "You mean, you know him, he's still alive?" Yes, dear. He is living more. Jack Kerouac twenty years ago, Richard Brautigan in the 1960s, many younger writers have fattened on his ease and rumble. In 1979 the daring, darling young man is a defiant aging one, both mellow and unmellow. The eyes are shrewd and full of dark looks. The body is hefty and quick. The mind is swift. Maybe there are third acts in American writing, but the public doesn't want to come back after the intermission.

A magazine editor once told me about assigning Saroyan to write an evocative piece about Tijuana. Fine, excellent, okay; next morning he returned to the editor's office with the completed essay. No, no, said the editor, we want you to go there; *then* we want you to write about it. Saroyan explained that he was saving them the expense money; he was willing to split the difference with them; he didn't need the trip. "And you know what?" the editor said, "It was a damn good piece. But that's not how it's done around here."

What he writes about his former wife is full of grief and regret. What she says about him is full of anger. Well, he's not easy, and he has unfair access to a dramatic imagination and wit and the continually replayed tape of injury in a rememorating genius. This is not the kindly Armenian raconteur. To go through marrying and divorcing twice, this couple must have suffered both love and trouble in earnest. His only daughter, Lucy, wanting to be an actress or a model or something, lives in London. His only son, Aram, used to write one-word poems, and made something of a scandal with them (father famed for using lots of words). Aram has recently published a book, *Genesis Angels,* about a destroyed American poet, Lew Welch. Father wishes his children well, would like to see more of them, wrote—in *Here Comes There Goes You Know Who* (chapter 48)—an excruciating few pages about a quarrel between father and son. It's not the Saroyan of *The Human Comedy,* but it is an American theme, simple, despairing, unforgettable.

About ten years ago, Saroyan told me he had given up gambling, source of some of his financial floundering. But then we disagreed about something, I forget what, and he said jubilantly, "I'll bet you." "I thought you'd given up gambling, Bill." "It isn't gambling if I win." In those days, he still roistered a bit, debating whether or not God was a horse, enlisting passersby in theological dispute, in the intermissions between his silent sad retreats in Paris, writing a couple of books a year (they're not all published), reading the newspaper that was his tablecloth, opening cans of fish and crunching baguettes, slowly paying his debts.

He wrote a book during this time entitled *Not Dying.* The spirit of it was that of Tolstoy's last diaries, when all had gone wrong—wife, children, religion, body—but the defiant old man ended almost every day's entry with the words: *"Still alive."*

Now, in his seventy-first year, Saroyan is still alive and not dying. He has written an astonishing new book. He has his irascible fun. He loves children and old folks and himself. That's how it's done around here.

Ethan Gold, making a drawing of Saroyan, suddenly said, "Oh, I made a booboo!" and Saroyan commanded him most imperatively, "Don't cross it out, just go on, booboos are very important and true." He asked Ethan to sign and date his portrait.

In Fresno, and again in San Francisco this spring—lunch at the Palace Court, a celebrational haunt from the old days—we talked about telling stories and novels, and I allowed as how I believe in rewriting. Saroyan allowed as how the subject has come up now and then; occasionally editors have poked at him with the notion that one might take thought and afterthought and different colors of pencil and paper and scissors and chop and rearrange and cut. With *Obituaries*, he decided to give it a try, but then he read the completed manuscript and it seemed just right the way it was. He shrugged and turned those dark soulful eyes on me and asked for another glass of tea and waited for me to dispute him.

Without reading the book, what could I say? But now I have read it, and I think he knows his proper business. Some (myself included) might want to edit, cut, collect, organize the tides of his voice. We can pick out the funny, the insightful, the astonishing stabs of knowledge, the griefs within the celebrations; deep matters astonish us, hidden in the charm and ebullience. It is generous of William Saroyan, still writing several books and plays and many stories a year, to offer us this treasure orchard in which the generations will forage.

IV
Language and Lingo, Art and Style

8
Hunting the Wild Bromide

Did you have fun in Paris?" I asked the neighbor lady, who has conducted her education not in books, classes or studies, but in "groups."

"Oh, wow! Just loved that café subculture," she stated, meaning that she liked to drink coffee on sidewalk terraces.

Brain-damaged sociology is one of the prime sources of what we might name Instant Bromide—the soporific word or phrase that, in a miraculous misconception, is born dead from overuse the very first time it is used.

Many years ago, in that brief shining moment between the beat and the hip eras in San Francisco, I was walking down Russian Hill one spring evening to take my dinner and met an acquaintance, an actor, who asked, "Hey, you look kind of uptight today, Herb?" (This was a statement in the form of a question, the unspoken prayer being: will you help me pass some time?) A few steps further along through the subculture, another friend said, "You see Ronnie back there? Really uptight about something." And down in North Beach, a *prix-fixe* political analyst at The Brighton Express remarked, "The President is getting super-uptight about Viet Nam."

I believe that fine June day saw the birth of uptight in the world. Three uptights came to roost in less than an hour, a phrase or word or grunt new to the anxious air. It was one of the first instant bromides of the flower age, and it illustrates a curious fraying of the American language—impoverishment by the process of enrichment, removal of meaning by the adding of meanings, the use of linguistic invention in order to make linguistic banality. Before the soap goes in, these words are already in the rinse cycle. Gold's Law: the rubber-stamp expression is a rubber stamp even the first time it is pressed into our brains.

In the never-ending search for new ways to say the same old things, the graduates of est are perhaps the current California champs. A Christmas card I received from a casual acquaintance reads:

*Your participation in my life
has added great value to it.
I look forward to our
celebrating and enjoying
the game of life together
in 1979.*

During the previous year, I had added great value to his life by taking him to lunch once in order to ask him some questions for an article I was writing. Our celebration and enjoyment of the game of life (two cheeseburgers and a couple of bottles of beer) was expense-accounted to *The New York Times Magazine*.

The telephone operators at est use the word *assist*, not help, as in: "This is Bonnie, how may I assist you?" The word *space* has become a free-floating symbol of belongingness, a kind of signal to others, without precise significance or with a precisely fudged significance. My first contact with this term came out of a bit of gossip from an est executive: "Last weekend Werner fired the whole board of directors."

"Fired them?" I asked.

"No, I misspoke myself. I mean he gave them their space to resign in."

Many other perfectly respectable words—*share, human, acknowledge* and *experience*, for example—have become part of the basic jargon of the time. Werner Erhard has a talent for taking words which have meaning in other contexts, such as *love* and *hunger*, and making them codes for membership in a special circle of the elect. (*Gut level* served this function light-years ago, when arguments first had thrust and disturbing voices at countercultural events were *lovingly ejected. Autres temps, autres groupes.*)

The story goes that Pinocchio's nose got longer with each lie he told. I wonder if it might also get swaybacked under the weight of bromide, and if this might account for the odd, pendulous construction of the nose of Richard Nixon. Let me make one thing clear; I don't mean to attack an emeritus leader of the free world in a dirty, underhanded way, like some of my enemies do, but I want to say this about that: perhaps the habit of instant bromide tends to break down cartilage when it is not destroying bone and moral fiber.

Or am I paranoid? (Translation: mildly disapproving or uneasy.)

The Chinese are international experts in instant bromide, winning the Standing Outdoor Mushmouth Olympics with the establishment of a "democracy wall" for the exhibition of friendship-type notes and memos. Of course, translation from the détente Mandarin may be the culprit here.

There is also a gray area of terms which seem to mean something hard to name by other nouns, as in the newly popular *single parent*. One scratches one's head to find another way of saying this, and yet, hearing a him or a her utter the words, "I'm a single parent," gives a person a feeling best described as icky (boarding-school jargon circa 1950). Often the instant bromide is a short and useful way of saying something—as *input* for information or *interface* for connection or *café subculture* for coffee drinkers are not. And yet perhaps the most loyally upfront language might not always serve the best. I would treasure the single parent more who says simply, "I'm raising my child alone," for the language too is forever a sturdy but sensitive child to be nurtured.

An advanced-thinking friend was recently engulfed by marital miseries. Like most of us in that storm, he talked, talked, talked. I was listening (giving him the space to talk in), but finally asked: "Does this mean you're going to get divorced?"

He stopped and thought a moment. "I'm neither going to get divorced nor not get divorced. I'm going to ride with the flow."

Oh-oh. His pain was evident, his grief was real, but his thought was pop Zen. He had searched in his heart for meaning and truth and he had returned with Alan Watts. I looked at my friend—uptight, seeking to find his space, oppressed by the game of life—and wondered how I might assist him.

Perhaps by saying nothing. But does not silence itself tend to become benign neglect? Is there any escape? Perhaps all we can do is speak for ourselves, listen for what we really think and then say it, and not try to please gurus or express allegiances or establish clans ("peer affiliations") with that ambiguous tool and blessing, the word.

Have a nice day, now. It would be Mickey Mouse not to.

9
Creatively Writing the Grippingly Erotic True Story

"My job was to be faithful to other women's men," she said, and I thought her brilliant and terrific. This lovely young person had a story to tell. She had lived it with her body, and now her way to justify it was to write it. She aroused my interest. For reasons which she named as curiosity plus money she had committed herself to a career as a white slave in a house in San Francisco. "Not a call girl, not a hooker," she said with winsome pedantry. "I was a white slave."

"I think thereupon might hang a tale," I said.

"You will help me bring it to the public?"

"Tell me, tell me," I said. "But you should write it, and I'll help you *after* you write it—you yourself, telling your own story. In the meantime, coffee?"

"I think I might," she said.

She was sleek, neat, tanned, dark, of that black-Irish darkness and bony nose which suggests Spain; and her body was exercised with loving care by herself and perhaps others;

and if I had to find a flaw because otherwise I might be too shy with her, it would be the shudder of cheek when she shook her head, a suggestion of jowls in her post-menopausal years—something I would surely never live to see. This would have to do for defect; it was all I could find.

Oh, and perhaps an extra portion of self-love in the pertness on the edge of the chair, so much boiling energy for what she wanted. Well, even I can't call that a flaw. But if I had been younger, her age, the incipient jowl might have made me fall helplessly, hopelessly, in love with her. She would have seemed possible, accessible. But since she was a mere child of twenty-three, one year out of UCLA, I only fell wistfully . . . Well, I coveted her distant loveliness, melting in the future like the lip of snow on the windowsills of my ancient childhood in Cleveland.

She explained that *Waiting for Cordelia,* my novel about callpersons in San Francisco, made her realize that I am just the one to guide her literary career. Praise makes me purr; I turned strict to control it. We met at Just Desserts. I thought young people and carrot cake and cappuccino would be more . . . counterphobic? is that the word?—than drinks in a darkened romantic bar. The bright, Danish and San Francisco, friendly coffee house was a straightforward environment for literary guidance. I could see better here, too.

"How did it happen?" I asked.

"Oh, a stupid summer marriage. Bored. Curious. And I want to write."

"I can understand that," I said soothingly.

"Also a little money never hurts."

"That too I understand," I said, and at this point I did not cover her small white hand with my big brown one. So much sagacity earned a fatherly pat, but even from this I abstained.

"You're such a good listener. People say you're . . ." she said, her voice trailing off. She didn't want to flatter me too much. But I got the idea.

"What was it, can you tell me, point of view?" I asked briskly.

"Well, some of the johns were nice. They weren't cripples and freaks as you might believe. I actually liked some of them. I like sex, by the way."

"Hmm, yes, very good," I said.

"And the madam was okay, too. A nurse. An R.N. from Phoenix. The place was clean. A detail: We couldn't read during working hours. We just had to wait in the parlor and look sexy. They gave us the clothes—bathing suits before five, kind of frilly gowns after dark—another detail."

"Not very *real*, is it?" Oh dear, when I'm nervous I get stupid.

She forgave me. "Reality isn't their shtick. For real love, you go outside. There's always the real world. This is kinks for normal people, you understand?"

"You have a great grasp of the picturesque detail," I said, "I seem to see an intensely dramatic and perhaps ironic . . . when you write it I'll be glad to help. Let's meet as soon as you do."

"I'd say I'm eighty percent there," she said.

"The experience is interesting in itself. That's half the battle."

"Since I was an alleged hooker," she said.

"What? You admit it, you're writing about it."

"Never convicted or even arrested, mister."

"Adolph Hitler, the suspected dictator? the accused tyrant? I see your point."

"Thank you," she said, "though wicked sarcasm never wins fair lady. Actually, I have a point, and it makes me mad. I'm thinking of going into paralegal work when I begin to lose my looks. Unless this writing deal goes down, in which case, I'll become an investigative reporter."

She pronounced investigative very well. She had a degree in speech from the University of California at Los Angeles. She didn't mean to quibble, her body's oratory sang, although her words quibbled a bit. The music of her face, that sulkiness and willfulness, that silken cajoling look, suddenly changed to fun: "I know how to do dirty things. Don't think I just learned them for work."

"Put that in."

"What?"

"In your story. Write it."

"Oh, man, I suppose you're right," and she laughed again, and it was as if the brooding never existed, and then she looked at me with desire—desire not for me but to be a writer—and asked: "It's hard, isn't it?"

"Yes. It's work. That's why it's fun, too."

She sighed. "Don't I know that story," she said.

The action here, I went away thinking, is going to be around the performance of literary criticism. And that was fine with me. For in this way I could be sure she was pure, I was clean, and our association would develop, as a man's and woman's must in these days, through a shared enterprise; in this case, the non-sexist one of helping her write the story of her servitude. I would avoid thinking too deeply in the implications.

She was curing herself through knowledge.

I was restoring a distracted soul to a new life as a new journalist.

But I said it was better not to think too much about the implications, didn't I? I went home and slept the sleep of the prospectively just. I took this rest on account.

She called a day later. She called *me*. My heart lifted. "I'm about ninety percent there," she said.

"Fine. Let's meet when you've finished."

A few days later: "I'm ninety-nine percent there."

"Ninety-nine?"

"Misspellings, punctuation, it's been so long since I was at UCLA."

"That's good enough. We meet. You bring Xerox."

"Suppose I just drop it off and then you call me when you've read it?"

"Oh. Okay. Any time."

"And then you call me," she said. "We'll bring it up to a hundred . . . together . . ."

Who knows where the devil a fellow might find true love? Why not with a girl who practices the writing trade?

So it was with a thrill that I returned home from dinner with a friend in North Beach to find the envelope with my name on it plus her initials: L.A. Lydia Alsop. It sounded like a real name to go with her real feelings, not the pseudonym one gives an editor or a john. And so I took off jacket and shoes, poured a cup of ginseng tea for myself, and read:

Who would ever guess that I, an upper class girl, raised in the heart of Westwood, California, with parents who loved me dearly and provided for my every need, would soon be laboring as a "hooker"—whore or prossie, though I prefer "White slave"—in a "Victorian-style" San Francisco sexual emporium? . . .

Oh dear. There were problems with the lead. The rhetorical question is a bit heavy, and the crowding of information, and the pinkie-pointed cuteness of the prose; and with this overuse of "quotation marks," could CAPITALIZATION be far behind? And hyperactive punctuation? No. For down a few more lines I found the short and dramatic paragraph:

Could I do this? NO!!!

When she described her first "john" (her quotation marks) as "a tall, attractive blond," I knew there was also some feminism in here someplace. Women who refer to a man as "a blond" or "a dark, swarthy, but intelligent brunette" are usually making several points more than mere description of hair and skin color. I am capable of falling in love quickly, also out of love, and this was one of those cases. However, I am addicted to the language and to teaching. So I read on with red pencil in hand.

I noted that she should not describe people five times, as she did, as "attractive." An attractive junior college graduate . . . the attractive visiting nurse . . . an attractive Asian person . . . No. Dramatize, I commanded, make the reader see. Don't tell us what you think; give the reader the information which enables him to think and feel. Objective Correlative (I would explain about T. S. Eliot's critical point). Cognitive Dissonance (I would explain about the theory of brainwashing applied to literary art). Visualize. Make smells. Participate in the drama of the situation so that we are surprised by developments. Reveal your own character and that of your cohookers; don't merely summarize. Put this work through the loom again.

In other words, the love system had been replaced in me by the pedagogical one. But who knows if perhaps they are not related?

The telephone rang and it was Lydia. "What percent am I there?" she asked.

"Would you like to come over and we'll talk about it? I just finished reading."

"Aw gee thanks, that was really neat of you. What percent?"

"Well, I think when you talked with me it was really interesting. Often people can tell a story better than they write it, they tense up, they think their words have to be ... Well, I can't explain, but the flash in your eyes and how you smiled communicated something to me—"

"Wah? Wah you say?"

"I can explain if I show you my squiggles on your manuscript."

"You wrote on it in *pen?*"

"It's a Xerox. Anyway, you need to do a lot of work—"

"I wanted to show it to a friend. Now he won't be able to read it—oh, shit. Okay, when can I pick it up?" She paused. "I mean I'm really grateful and I want to hear all you have to say, but I was hoping you would help me sell it to *Playboy* or *Esquire* or one of them, maybe *Ms.* But I'm coming over."

She was dressed for a conference, and again that heart-stopping loveliness. This is a metaphor; she didn't stop my heart; she raised my blood pressure with a little jolt. She was wearing pale horn-rimmed glasses that played enticingly against her glossy dark hair, her skin, her damp, soft, innocent mouth. I tried to recall how I had recently fallen out of love, due to prose. Now I was backsliding. "Rhetoric," I said. "Grammar. Syntax. Spelling. Coffee or ginseng tea?"

"You got anything to drink?"

"Scotch, vodka, gin."

"Whatever's right. Oh, scotch on rocks, you probably don't have any soda."

"That's the kind of insight we need in the piece," I said. "You're right, I don't carry the mixes."

As we settled down with the manuscript, I noticed a little

lovely lithe dancer's twist of her waist. A delight. More delightful if it wasn't straining to look at my clock which was busily ticking away her valuable time. In my heart of hearts I began to wonder if she would listen to literary criticism if I offered to pay her fifty dollars to do so. "If you'd rather not talk about your piece, we could just talk," I said.

"No, no, I came here for that, I'm really . . ." That heartbreaking little smile. "I'm really interested, Herb. Critique away."

And so I delivered myself of a few general comments: Frank, complete, open. Explore the whole creative writing approach. Understand that the reader knows nothing, may not even be interested, but you must interest him by engaging his attention. A kind of teasing, a kind of play. And good speech, Lydia, I explained, I mean good writing, tends to reflect good speech. "In real life you have a way of letting people know what you feel, and of getting their attention. You need to do this in your prose."

"Body English," she said. "My little moves. My forehand, my backhand. How I speak is with my little moves."

"Yes, yes, yes, but something of that is in good writing. It's almost a metabolic thing. Your writing style reflects your blood, your heart, your nervous system, how you digest and breathe—"

She began to look at me as if I were a freak who had freaky needs. She didn't like men who talk dirty (that was in the piece).

"Like when you describe your 'Patty Hearst Trip.' I mean, all in white, frills, a child's bed, dolls, and you tell them you're sixteen years old. That's a good incident. But I can imagine you doing that because I know you. The reader doesn't know you. You have to see the room, the furniture, what he says, what you say, what you do . . . I mean cuddle.

I mean are you wearing perfume? I mean—well, it's your story."

She was thoughtful. She put down the drink. "You mean I have to make it more commercial?" she asked.

"That's a way of putting it. I mean you have to live through it more deeply."

"I was wearing Blue Grass cologne. Estelle gave it to me, it was her idea, I thought it was yucchy stuff."

"That's what we need to know. And tell about you and Estelle. You have to make it more dense, more vivid, you have to give us the details, exactly what happens."

Lydia smiled that heartbreaking corrupt smile at me, and having finished her glass and heard me out, arose with the graceful motion of a dancer; strong and practiced knees. A smile makes up for a lot. "I always knew," she said, "an old guy like you—you're not so old, but I mean in his heart—I mean it takes someone who's been through what I have to appreciate my writing."

My reading skills were on the line. I loved her a lot less now. I no longer saw the incipient jowl, but I saw an argument. "You mean a limited audience of ex-hookers?" I asked. "I don't know if there's an alumni journal, my dear."

"You're trying to be funny, I can see that. You're trying to be sarcastic. Well, it only shows one thing." She picked up her manuscript. She held it by the neck. "You try, it proves," she said, "you try to break into a new field and the folks who are already there, they have the ins, they know the editors, they won't let you. But I'm not going to talk dirty for anyone."

10
Movies for Teevee—The Pride and the Money, The Sorrows and the Aggravation

Is it possible to credit a legend which goes all the way back to the early fifties? Perhaps not; geological strata of Nielsen ratings lie impacted on history, the old shows imbedded in the shale. But everyone *knows* the story is true—that the MGM top brass threatened summary dismissal of any executive found with a teevee set on studio premises. And one was so caught! However, he made an impassioned plea for his job. He kept the set in his offices, he explained, only to stick pins in it. This voodoo calmed the querulous minds which were proclaiming that Movies Are Better Than Ever; ergo, Go Out to a Movie Tonight.

He kept his job. He is now an Important Executive, a Founding Father.

The scratched, pricked, and tortured television set was thrown in a litter heap.

But a beginning had been made in the non-banishment of television from the movie business. Production which had been centered in New York—remember Rod Serling, Paddy Chayefsky, Robert Alan Aurthur, their lyrical-passionate-realistic Manhattan original plays?—was beckoned home by the wizards of ooze. The studios couldn't beat it, so they joined it. And in the fullness of time the Movie of the Week was born. (I leave out some of the intervening begats.)

Let us now begin this ramble through the wonderful world of teevee movies with a few pre-questions which are really, like most rhetorical questions, statements:

How the box shapes the intentions of the moviemakers. How the intimacy of the form suits the intimacy of family viewing. How costs reduce. How mass, onetime, non-critical-feedback inundation of the market makes for broad attack: The *TV Guide* advance notice takes the place of the Pauline Kaels of the world. How the accessibility of the snap-off button means that the pace must hold, hold, hold, *grip* the viewer. How you have to build your energy not to satisfy Aristotle's unities but to keep the viewer on channel through the commercials.

In a theater, the couple that pays six or eight dollars for tickets—and maybe a babysitter besides, and maybe cab or parking—won't walk out and head down the block. There is time to engage their attention. They are sharing the communal experience. Here in Sony territory, that private global village, the action must regularly peak and breathe something like suspense so that the viewer won't switch off during the Buick or Kleenex or Binaca break.

In the living room, someone can say, "Dad, let's go to Channel 7." Or more likely Dad, without asking, will just flip to Channel 7, because he *knows.* Taste is instantaneous here.

Look for some answers to these questions in the next segment of this scenario. And also look for some questions to these answers.

There is a certain serendipity in the making of any film, even the speeded-up teevee version, in which the director functions less as "auteur" than as traffic cop ("cop de trafique"). I was at Van Nuys Airport in Burbank, watching the Israeli commando team run through its stuff in "Raid on Entebbe" and noticed a young black extra from Watts among the Israeli commandos. Why him?

"Accident, I guess," said a production assistant.

"Federal law requires it," said an assistant director.

I asked the extra himself, chic in his commando uniform with Hebrew markings. "Man, I never been in no movie before. Twenty-five dollars plus two meals. It's groovy, man."

Said Edgar J. Scherick, the producer: "In the lighting we use, nobody'll see him."

Said the Israeli technical expert, a young man with an M.A. in Film from the University of Southern California: "Of course, there are black Jews in Israel . . ."

At the outdoor lunch on trays, catered from a truck—and this Air National Guard base at Van Nuys Airport brought back no nostalgia at all for my own years in the Air Force—I sat with John Saxon, Jack Warden, the Israeli technical expert, Irvin Kershner, the director of the film, and some of the extras. Kibbitzing, meddling, just passing the time, I urged Kershner to highlight the black commando. "Kind of an interesting idea," he said. "We don't need a line for him. Just let the camera see him, no comment, let the viewer reason it out."

And so our perception of history could be altered by the accident of a casting director saying to an adventurous kid who just bopped down to Burbank from Watts: "Yeah, *you.*" In front of the blue boxes with our beer and chips and fantasies, we look at the screen and have an insight about Israeli society. Correct? Incorrect? Accident? Pure fancy? Fate declares itself through a casting hazard, a director's impulse. Or perhaps the producer just edits Fate out.

Charles Bronson, whose price is one million dollars per picture, doesn't normally make movies for teevee. His presence in "Raid on Entebbe" guaranteed it an important sale in Europe. I asked why he was doing this film.

"Why am I doing it?" he asked cautiously in return.

He was wearing his Israeli general's uniform. His Charles Bronson's chauffeured black Mercedes was idling nearby. The moral pressure for someone to speak was overwhelming. He won the battle of silence. I said: "You like the story. You like the money. You have the time."

He thought that one over. "I like the story," he said. "The money was right." He suddenly turned the full glare of his face upon mine. "What do you mean, I have the time? You think I work too much?"

Later I asked a production assistant about Bronson's special status. His stance expresses power and a tense self-esteem. "Is he aware of his prerogatives?"

"He's not aware of anything *but* his prerogatives. He refuses to admit this is a teevee movie."

In other words, the huge sums paid him guarantee huge sums in return, and that gives him a certain authority, and everyone knows it. It counts in the movie world. It counts in the movie-for-teevee world. He may not look like General Shomron. He is much older than General Shomron. He pronounces the word *agin,* meaning one more time, in a way more suitable to a shoot-em-up Western than an Israeli general planning a commando raid. But he looms large on the small and big screens.

"Twentieth Century-Fox, which was flat on its back, has climbed triumphantly onto its knees, thanks to movies-for-TV."—A network philosopher.

"Raid on Entebbe" is an elaborate production. Talent and

luck are taking hold to break out of the mold of hamburger teevee product. It's fun to watch it in action—Peter Finch, John Saxon, Jack Warden, the young actor who plays Yohanaton, Yaphet Kotto, who plays Idi Amin, Horst Buchholz, who contacted the German mother of the terrorist he plays . . . And Irvin Kershner, the director, up all night rewriting a pedestrian action script . . . And the murder of the Warner Bros. Entebbe movie when Bronson came aboard . . . The magic of the business is that it still provides surprise, excitement, peculiar twists and turns, fun. Yes, there is fun: red-eyed all-night encounters and straining to put all the pieces together.

Hal Landers, normally a producer of buy-your-ticket movies, was now producing "Relentless" as a teevee movie. Why? He owned the property. He couldn't get it done in the expensive form. He wanted to get it done. His budget is about $850,000. "It's a dog's life without a leash," he says. "Making a movie for teevee is like trying to cook a soufflé with a match."

Landers, producer, and Alan Meyerson, director of both teevee and theatrical movies, utter words of modest self-deprecation: the future is not for the artist in teevee. Occasionally there is an "Autobiography of Miss Jane Pittman," which advanced John Korty's career, and perhaps Alex Haley's "Roots" or "Raid on Entebbe" will be landmarks, make some kind of unfading news; but usually: "It's as good as you can make it," the poignant Landers said, "and that's the end of it."

"You can't make it very good," said Meyerson. "You have a scene where someone says he's going to the store and the next scene is in Havana. You don't even have time to write in a line that says, 'I'm going to the store in Havana.' "

"There's no life's blood in it," said Landers. "There's passion in this real film I'm preparing now, a blockbuster, I can't tell you what it is." (He told me, but I promised.) "In a teevee film, you think: Okay, we'll get some money in the foreign sales."

Time, money, energy, passion, shooting schedules: A movie is expensive detail work, a mosaic of elements, but a teevee movie has to be a rapid sketch. The director usually walks in and some accountants have said: Here are your actors, your script, your sets, your costumes. The director is down the line in importance. The traffic cop's job is to say: Move here, move there. In a real movie, despite all the nonsense of "auteur" theory, the director really does oversee things, make decisions, knit it together in the light of his own conception. Korty did it with Miss Jane Pittman, but that's a rare exception. Teevee movies are not made for good reviews, building an audience. They are made to captivate some viewers *right now*. They are made to keep millions of people steady for the commercials *right now*. They are made for right now.

So action, a few viable names, a rapid comprehensibility are required. Even if John Leonard or your local teevee columnist gives it a great review, this good boon comes after the showing and no one is going to turn back the time machine to applaud the critic's judgment. Reruns happen, of course. But they have to do with ratings, not with a nice column in a newspaper. With a film-for-theater, the nice review or word of mouth brings people in and an audience can build. By the time word gets around for a teevee movie, the box is flickering with another tale.

Some teevee movies survive, of course, as pilots of series. What looks like a movie is really a tryout of characters, mood, style, actors, a complex intermeshing of popular possibilities. And so the spin-off, the series, the attachment to a continuing story which probably shouldn't be compared with the interest in Dickens, as so many like to do in that way they have. The pilot is the Honored Ancestor of the series.

Seeking understanding, one might make this equation: Teevee movies are to bigscreen films as pulp fiction used to be to quality/slick/art fiction. And just as honest pulp—say, Dashiell Hammett or Ross Macdonald—crosses surreptitiously over into the art world, so there are surprises which suddenly appear in the blue non-Pandora's box. They are legendary. They often win prizes. They are cited about how "television movies have come of age" (frequent popular expression at CBS, circa 1970). They are rare.

Triumph is rare in the quality/slick/art world, also. The difference in filmmaking is that the money really matters; you need money to take care of cutting, editing, sets, costuming. Size of screen and rhythm of movement really matter; you can't easily break a masterpiece for frequent commercials. Movies are a group art form and the group must eat, must work together, must have time. Little time, little work, little eat means littler work. Or so everyone I talked with in my tours of studioland have informed me.

"It All Happens So Fast" might serve as the title of a study of teevee movies. Ray Aghayan, costume designer, renews the familiar theme: "In television, it all happens so fast. I may have four days to think about it, and a week to do it. When I do a feature film, there's time." John Saxon says: "The difference between teevee and real movies? Many months."

I detect rue.

Alan Factor, a former actor now producing films for teevee, says, "Reviews and word of mouth mean nothing. They come out *after*. The main consideration is the review in *TV Guide*, which is a selling proposition, based on preselling, star value." There's a bit of Alice in Wonderland in this conception: first the verdict, then the show. Another sort of preselling, of course, is the selling to the advertisers, who look for a structure which builds to carry the viewer through the commercial without tapping his feet, switching his channel. "Getting the deal, man," says Factor, "means getting the networks to agree. The ways of financing are limited." In other words, though he didn't say this, it all has something to do with the products sold on television. This may be a profound surprise to no one.

Factor and his partner, John Newland, are doing a film-for-teevee in February. They have done them in the past. They sounded somewhat subdued in preproduction. They cross the river of product by jumping from half-submerged rocks, rock to rock, and not looking back.

Commercial Break

The PBS television outlet in Los Angeles carried a sensitive and delicate documentary based on the work of an anthropologist who had studied a poverty-stricken neighborhood of old Jews. The film examined their social, personal, religious lives, focused about a community center, and showed them as indomitable, testy, charming, pathetic. They were survivors.

Enter a producer of movies-of-the-week. He sees a group of antic old folks, cute personality kids, with lovable conflicts and picturesque habits. A subject for a teevee movie here! Also, and more to the point, since the cast of characters is locked into a permanent scene, maybe a series! "Will you take a meet?" he asks the filmmaker and anthropologist. The producer tells them he sees magic, he feels it, he can almost taste it. The documentary is wonderful. He smells audience, humanity, ratings. Who could want more?

Nobody.

There is only one problem. "Do these people *have* to be Jewish?"

The filmmaker and the anthropologist are stunned. The central issue was the specific kind of community, the holy days, the sabbaths, the shared memories and allegiances.

Silence. "No," the anthropologist replies. "They don't even have to be old."

"They don't even have to be human," chimes in the filmmaker. "They could be geriatric bionic people."

It is not a fruitful meet.

Another Commercial Break

A writer I know had an idea for a movie-for-teevee. It concerned a varied group of divorced fathers who vacation with their children in a rundown seaside resort. A pair of producers picked it up and said, "Touching! Real! Deeply human! Will you take a meet? Can we run with it?" They ran to a major network. A network producer asked to "take a meet" with the writer. The writer came to Los Angeles and the meeting was took.

The network producer said: "I like it. I'm Catholic and I've been divorced. I like it a lot. The horror of it. The today of it. Gentlemen, I like it one hundred and ten percent."

The three petitioners—two producers and one writer—went out to a pasta palace on La Cienega to celebrate with the usual overeating. The writer called his agent to make sure he would get top dollar; in this case, perhaps as much as $30,000 or $35,000 for writing the script. (The price can go as low as $15,000. It can go higher.) They had a good dinner. Cigars. Wine. Pre-celebration. They waited.

The network called. The meat computer said: "It's a wonderful idea. You boys are the boys to do it. We like it a lot. We're not going to do it."

"Uh, why?"

"It should be made, it's a surefire prizewinner, we don't think it'll get the ratings."

Public Service Announcement

An example of the Working Actor, typical of the movie-for-teevee performer at his best, is John Saxon, giving another of his strong, carefully thought-out performances as General Pelod in "Raid on Entebbe." Originally Saxon was discovered by the same agent who discovered (and named) such as Tab Hunter, Rock Hudson, during the time of funny made-up names. A teenage model in New York, he became a heartthrob of the fifties in such movies as *High School Confidential.* But he was serious about acting. He appeared in movies directed by John Huston; he appeared opposite Marlon Brando. He took singing lessons. He studied Tai Chi. He worked out. He read. He received good notices when reviewers looked beyond the dark, Italian, un-Saxon-like good looks. Nevertheless, he has not yet become one of the bankable luminaries, who today are represented by Brando, Newman, Redford, Warren Beatty. And so he began appearing in movies-for-teevee, in parts ranging from brooding lover to brooding killer, from patient curator of souls to snarling psychotic. He also went on doing roles in feature films; he too is popular in Europe. He likes working, month in month out; he is reliable; directors like working with him; it is known that he gives good value; he is an acting actor. How does it pay? He makes a Lot of Money.

Surely he would like to find a big property, the sort of thing Warren Beatty did with *Bonnie and Clyde,* and be one of those lazy superstars, super bankable, instead of being a mere wealthy, hardworking, successful movie-for-teevee star. So would Elizabeth Ashley. So, for that matter, would Louise Lasser. Teevee is not quite, oh, traveling first class in the firmament. But it requires workmen and its workmen do what the hire needs to have done.

TEEVEE FILMS—A FACT AND RUMOR SHEET

Budgets

Because the subject of money is made of gas in Los Angeles, and follows the laws of thermodynamics, and floats away with irreal iridescence through the smog, what follows is hearsay, a collection of informed judgments, sometimes contradictory. ("Do I contradict myself?" asked Walt Whitman. "Very well, then I contradict myself.") Budgets are inflated to make profits, cover overheads, deny participation to participating artists. Budgets are rarely deflated. Caveat emptor.

In the usual format of the usual so-called movie of the week, the budget floats in the lower end of a $450,000–$600,000 spread. There are other variants. For reasons of special hopes or pressures, girlfriends or ego trips, movies like "Love among the Ruins" have been made for more. Some specials are made for more. The Xerox Corporation will go all out now and then. Many are *claimed* to be made for more (pseudo-Xeroxes). It is curious to compare these figures against the rental fees paid by the networks for theatrical features released on teevee. These vary, of course, depending on the venerability of the film, viability of the stars (or "factors"), previous theatrical success. NBC paid five million dollars ($5,000,000) for *one* screening of *Gone With the Wind.* Between $300,000 and $1,000,000 are common sums.

Film budgets are divided into two components—"below the line" and "above the line" costs. "Above the line" costs include story and script, producer fees, director fees, main player fees. "Below the line" costs include everything else through delivery of a negative to the studio, including the mysterious "overhead" factor, so beloved by accountants. For a teevee movie, a minimum "above the line" (hereafter used without quotation marks) runs approximately:

Story and script	$15,000
Director	15,000
Producer	15,000
Main players (3)	40,000
	$85,000

Maximum movie-of-the-week figures might be double this.

Given this approximation, and assuming a total budget of $450,000, about $365,000 remains for the rest of the production. Typically, this would allow a shooting schedule of fifteen days at an average cost of about $22,000 per shooting day. Now we can introduce another element in the comparison with theatrical features: shooting ratio. This denotes the number of feet of film which will be shot in relation to the number of feet which will appear in the finished film. The "movie-of-the-week" format involves ninety minutes of film, eight thousand feet of film in the finished product. For theatrical features in studio work, a four to one or five to one ratio is acceptable; location work may go to twelve to one or even fifteen to one; some meticulous or profligate directors —Arthur Penn is famous for this—shoot as much as twenty or twenty-five to one to get exactly the choices and effects they want.

For a movie of the week, the director may be fired (sometimes is) for shooting at a ratio greater than three to one or four to one, including both studio and location work. "Zip zip, set up, shoot; zip zip, set up, shoot again," said one director. "I'm a goddamn traffic cop. Only goddamn traffic cops aren't fired for telling their name. I won't even give you my badge number."

The speed-up and economy affects the teevee film in several ways. An attempt is made to keep the work inside the studio as much as possible. The elements are under control; no planes suddenly coming in, no sudden changes of light. Also the director attempts to cram as much information into his master shot as he can. The master shot is often a composite, made in one single take, of a traditional master plus different angle coverage. This saves money in the form of footage cranked through the camera and labs. Perhaps more important, it saves time.

Format and Rhythm

Teevee films are a part of the teevee marketing and sales tool. They are not paid for by the viewer or by Aristotle, and consequently have less responsibility to the classical unities. The advertiser, the agency, the network, the studio are concerned with popularity, immediate lure, and a format which permits frequent interruption for the commercial. One might define the teevee playwright's form as follows: short scene, followed by irrelevant interruption, followed by short scene punchy enough to carry the viewer through the next irrelevant interruption, followed by short scene. . . . A variant is the pilot feature, made to introduce characters and situation to a broad audience. The original "The Waltons" was a CBS Christmas special with Patricia Neal, made with more care than the spin-off series. Patricia Neal disappeared from the series. Internal commercials appeared. If "Raid on Entebbe" were to become a series—gallant Israeli commandos strike again! again!—one could be sure that Charles Bronson would slip away in the night.

Another variant is the mini-series, which is our old friend

the Saturday afternoon serial, now grandly named "the novel of the screen." "Rich Man, Poor Man" might be made with greater gloss than other teevee movies.

And still another variant is represented in "Raid on Entebbe"—the hybrid film, made for television in this country, good enough for theatrical viewing abroad, and perhaps eventually for some theatrical viewing here, too. (This double reverse twist occurred with "Brian's Song.") Charles Bronson is a big star in Europe. Peter Finch and Irvin Kershner class-up the project. The budget and care can be increased accordingly. Better typewriters and bond paper don't significantly increase the yield of a poet or novelist. But the time and technical improvements bought by adequate money significantly change the possibilities of a technical and group medium like film.

Summing up the difference, a low budget ninety-minute theatrical film, costing say a million dollars (below the line, $750,000), might be on a shooting schedule of forty to forty-eight days. What it comes down to, for the director and the care he puts into it, is approximately 45 days to get his ninety minutes, against fifteen days for the teevee feature. The movie visited in your local Moorish palace is not necessarily three times as good as the one in the set at the foot of your bed. But the time difference is a significant element in the excellence of film.

Producers of movies-for-teevee are not always as articulate as other award-winning members of the human race. I asked a successful producer—a word which covers the functions of promoter, agent, accountant, censor, salesman, crybaby—how much one of his pictures cost. "Really," I said. "Don't jive me."

He paused, startled. He looked deep into my yellow-brown eyes. He said: "I can't just tell you that cold turkey."

Sidney Beckerman was visiting the set of "Raid on Entebbe" as a friend of the production. His son wrote the original script. The elder Beckerman, a good-looking, relaxed, curly-haired man, known to his friends as The Prince of Darkness, is a big-time producer. *Marathon Man* is an example of a big-time production. I asked him the most important difference between a big-time theatrical production and a movie for the small (though getting larger) screen. "Time," he said. "You don't have the leeway. The shooting schedule. The money. But here, of course, you get a Bill Butler, cinematographer for *Jaws,* you get an Irvin Kershner—that kind of energy. So you can cross over to big screen from here. You get all-stars, you double your shooting schedule, you have a hot item, you get Warner Brothers to abandon their Entebbe item, you don't necessarily shoot in Israel and Africa"—they're shooting "on location" in Burbank and Stockton—"but you do a biggish film anyway. Bronson makes it a theatrical feature in Europe."

"I know."

"I suppose people mention it to you. Well, there's an electricity that changes things."

The Entebbe rescuers stand tall and walk proud with Charles Bronson firming up their prospects.

On a day when I watched the filming of a scene at Van Nuys Airport—now the secret military airport in Israel—General Gur, played by Jack Warden, was demonstrating the planned landing at Entebbe to General Shomron (Charles Bronson), General Peled (John Saxon), and Colonel Yohanaton, played by Stephen Macht. Shooting had been delayed; they had worked until 4:00 A.M. the previous morning; a certain amount of coffee nerves. Extras—the Israeli commando team—were mosying about, reading *Variety* and munching tacos. The miniclimax of the scene comes when General Gur demonstrates the landing of the assault plane with a balsawood model on which a ten-cent wheel was supposed to come off (darting glances, consternation, menace). The toy plane was late getting there. The wheel didn't come off right. The problems of this long scene, which engaged hundreds of grown men and women, and a cost of perhaps not much under $100,000, exemplify the magic and pain, the sorrows and the aggravations, of any moviemaking. The producer was clutching his side (appendix? wallet?) and shouting: Do it differently, do something else! The director, Irvin Kershner, known as an intuitive perfectionist, was hitting his forehead, where the frontal lobe, filled with ideas, swells and meets the limits of bone. He wanted it done the right way, his way, the creative way, the exciting way. . . . It cost a lot.

"And that," said an assistant, as we watched through the long night, "shows this is not just another dumb movie for teevee. We're hanging that whole scene on waiting for the goddamn balsawood plane to act right. What else do you need to prove it's one hell of a major production?"

V
Life on the Brink

11
No Goddamn Body Stays Married Anymore

Husbands want oceanic union, eyes in eyes, heart touching heart, tongue on tongue, oceanic trust and faith and total understanding—and also a twenty-two-year-old body and teasing sexiness.

No wonder so many men spend the evenings with their pals.

Wives want a secure honest protective deeply-tanned chap with one hell of a lot of gentle goodies in his soul—and also they want to fulfill themselves through independence and an occasional adventure.

No wonder so many women spend the evenings raising their consciousness.

No wonder so many children shuttle back and forth, touring Great America or Marine World with dad and the birthday party-carpool map with mom. No wonder the seven-year-old son of a woman I dated for the first time said to me as we left for dinner: "Won't you come back and spend the night, please?"

Lonely kid. Lonely mother. Lonely me.

As well as we know that smoking leads to lung cancer (although not in each and every case) we know that marriage leads to divorce (although some sweetly breathe their last in the arms of the original teenage beloved). That divorce is an epidemic everyone knows. In California it's nearly a *rule.* Marriage, if it were a business venture, would be called the sure route to bankruptcy—let this be stipulated.

We can also agree that the usual explanations—married young, changed, got distracted, got bored—apply and don't apply, explain and don't explain enough. We can add that the new freedoms, the god-given right to life, liberty, and the pursuit of Growth, play a part. We enter the temple of marriage expecting everything, solution to all ills, multiplication of all pleasures. The arithmetic fades. Who marries is not the same person as the one who stays married. And there are two in this adventure of becoming. How can they be expected to change and grow together?

So love is as natural as the birds' singing. And divorce is as natural as the birds' pecking each other's eyes out.

Might it help to have other friends, even other lovers? Periods of vacation separately, recreations together? Open marriage, no questions? Refreshingly separate careers or nurturing common endeavors, as on a farm? Alternate lifestyles, group therapy, swinging weekends, tribal agglomerations?

It might. It sometimes seems to; the manuals tell us so. The celebrated authors of a book on open marriage succeeded in their own original, primal, revolutionary open marriage—and then got divorced. Well, maybe it was a happier, more creative and venturesome divorce, with more fun fistfights over who got custody of the Barca lounger. People decide it's not worth the struggle. Friends of mine in Marin County labored for years to save their marriage, and they grew and struggled and employed counselors for Gestalt sessions and developed innovative techniques and refreshed themselves and Rolfed and jogged and discussed absolutely everything in a rational manner and primal screamed, discussing everything in an irrational manner, and finally decided to get divorced.

"Why?" I asked. "Didn't it work?"

"Of course it did," he said.

"And we love each other forever, we're riding with the flow," she said.

"Wah?" I said.

"It worked," he said, "but you know? It just doesn't seem worth it."

This is not a joke. Freshness is what they were talking about. If you cure all the problems, you still have this one—*tuckered out*. The flow she mentioned is a mature sense that life brings changes, including changes together, and the vital connection for these two henceforeward will be the lack of connection. The excitement and vividness and sweetness of pain, doubt, panic, grief, mourning are sought in a time when the last frontier (drugs were a brief fad) is sex. Unless there are massacres, it's not a frontier. To conquer this vision of adventure and risk requires failure and success snatched from the jaws of the family room.

"We learned to love each other," she says, "a lot. But I want somebody new to learn with."

I'm not sure I like this. I even think I don't like it. But there it is. Permanence in more than the quest would be nice. But when so much is handed us, including sex, the dangerous plains and peaks of love and marriage must be kept unfair, difficult, unhanded to us. You would think death, imminent for everybody, would be enough experience of loss. Love used to be the reassuring answer to death —the loss of parents, friends, our own youth. Beyond all the nonsense stands a limit—our own mortality. We could keep it in balance with family, with children, and follow the rhythm of the years. Something could be permanent—marriage. But most of us can't wait for our extended youth to end in peace and have to find the crazed novelty of self-destruction before death. To divorce is to die a little. We seek inoculation, with grief, loss, mourning.

Is that too weighty? We also seek the throat-tightening ache, the heart-stopping rush of a new love. And we think it is our right to sustain this rebirth forever and ever. Repeat after me: this is our mistake.

The forlornness of life, the grief of loss (of what? mother and dad? of childhood? of life itself?) leads us to hope of renewal through a fresh sharing and courtship. Squeaky-clean hair and a perfect set of pectorals will not console us long for the lack of the right Other. We want to love anew —not only as if it were the first time, but also as if it will be the last time. We want to see the same way: afresh, anew, and finally at peace. We want to kiss and make love as a final statement to the court.

And then, after such a blather for permanence and meaning, we also want it to be fun.

No wonder we slip on the sly into the sack with the undiscovered person onto whom we can pour all these longings. Only a fantasy can gratify the fantastic. And only a person who finally becomes real, beyond those secret nights in the sack, those noonsies, those weekends at Sugarbush, can satisfy our real needs.

Marriage is no longer the only game in town. Both men and women have alternatives, and they are not all alcoholism, failure, frustration, suicide, and a wan old age walking the poodle and taking the turkey plate alone with quiet dignity on national holidays. Permanent youth, perpetual growth, stalwart adventures, erotic play are long-term possibilities brought to us all through the help of sport, vitamins, hair care, and regular exercise. Women have emancipated themselves and the fallout for men is interesting, too.

Nevertheless, the marriage frontier is still unexplored country; its risks and promises and rumors of trouble discourage us only sometimes. We are a race of explorers.

This group of furloughed-from-dope fruit flies from the sixties has been biting at me lately to join them in the holy institution of Polyfidelity. There's a sacrament, where you sing and dance and fuck everybody, and then there are rules: *only with people in the group.* Any other behavior results in angst, jealousy, expulsion, divorce from the Family.

"Come on, Herb, you can hack it. We got blondes and browns, we got kids and experienced old ladies. Man, we got almost twenty-five soulful folks in our commune, give or take a few flakes."

"I might try my own way of working it out."

"Try, man. You try. See what success Western Civilization brings you."

Amen to that anthem of failure. Nobody stays married anymore. Nuclear Marriage has been a bringdown. The young, the middle-aged, the seamy and worn all get divorced. We all know—let's stipulate this, too—that monogamy has not been a part of marriage for a long time; sexual freedom took the facts public. But the monogamous form, which means a monogamous intention, endured. Secrecy and hypocrisy were the homage paid a romantic ideal. That is, people had adventures, but they thought it was worth keeping children, house, and history intact in this process. At least they considered it. Women wanted security; men wanted security, too. They tried to accommodate to freedom by a little sneakiness, and then a little openness.

Neither one worked very well. Every open marriage I know has dissolved in horrific recriminations. He was allowed to fuck, but he couldn't *care* (after awhile he cared). She was allowed to fuck, but not *everybody* (she made it with everybody, and especially this Laguna Beach guitarist and she even started writing poems to him).

The end of the temporary smug contentment with sexual freedom came with the women's movement.

Let's get to that in a moment, but just to relieve the suspense: No, I don't think the women's movement is bad. It's revolutionary and it makes difficulties and it has sealed the fate of marriage in our time, but I'm not hostile to it. It was inevitable. It makes women interesting in a different way. But let's save that for later.

The seeds of change were sown by the uneasy alliance of romantic love with Christian or Married love. There was play and there was responsibility, a common enterprise and the kids to raise, and there was increasingly toward the twentieth century this touching effort to make the yoked spouses into lovers, too. Self-help sex books and the teasing of beauty and the long life of couples and the education of women and the decay of religion and the decline of village culture and you name it. In courtship you had romance; in marriage, regular sex; and the twain were supposed to meet.

It was an illusion. Men went to their secretaries or equivalent; women to the milkman or attractive neighbor; and serial monogamy was invented. Each tried once again if there was a painful divorce. Or they patched it up and lived a warring truce. Ugh, hypocrisy. And pain. And stifling. And so suburbs and wars and hobbies and ulcers and drink and a host of distractions relieved the couple of each other. Plus conventions and an occasional lucky wild meeting.

After World War II Americans started to say: We're going to get something more! And we sure did.

So there was this brief flowering of do it, do it, do it, and the euphoric shock on the part of men when it turned out that women—nice women, smart women, funny women, beautiful women—not just round-heeled women—also wanted to do it. In fact, loved it. In fact, demanded it.

Oh, wow.

But the early warnings were drowned in the general blissful playing of the sixties. After all, the world was coming apart, America was at war, the fumes of progress filled our lives, so do it. We'll figure out what it leads to later.

It got messy. It led to the breakdown of marriage. Okay, so what? It led to loneliness, heartbreak, isolation, and grief. It led to wobbly souls worrying about how to make the next day different from the today. Not just better, just different. It led to a nomadic quest for Esalen, Sandstone, Arica, est, brotherhood, sisterhood, selfhood, love as an oasis nobody could define.

Now don't tell me about how Middle America still makes it okay. Don't tell me this is only New York and L.A. and Chicago and San Francisco I'm talking about. My own roots are in the Middle West, and the postal service was busy, the telephone lines were busy, when I got divorced out here in tasty San Francisco.

I heard about how they were Catholic and they got divorced anyway. Or they didn't, and another kid on the way, I'm going nuts, what can I do?

I heard about how the property, the kids, the town of Lakewood, the way things are back here. So we're just going to make our arrangements. But you'd be surprised; they've got swinging fern bars in the Flats near downtown Cleveland, and on the West Side, and in Shaker Heights, too.

I heard from those who said it's just too crowded, it's dense, it's sad, it's lonely . . . Sad and lonely as I was, I heard from those who said it was sadder and lonelier in a claustrophobic marriage or a marriage without joy and excitement, only there is the difference: I could expect change, I could get well. They expected nothing but more of the same.

So those marriages will break up or they won't and it's smallscreen disaster time whichever. Middle America has been polished to the same high gloss as the hip coasts; double knit takes to ferns and misery as well as French jeans. As long as I'm feeling sorry for me, for the men and women like me, I might as well feel sorry for those others out there—who are also just like you and me. We get the same mads and midnight horrors and maybe even the same metabolic highs at the dream of love (*She* looked at me and it was unmistakable! *He* called!). My dentist friend, my real estate friend, my schoolteacher friend from Cleveland and Detroit and Chicago say: "Hey, is there some fun out here? Where is it?"

Their wives say the same thing.

Don't tell me marriage is still safe haven anyplace in America. Well, maybe among the Amish . . . a few Orthodox Jews or Christians . . . maybe someplace people talk about the Sanctity of the Condo.

When my white-shoed classmate from Lakewood (Ohio) High School comes lurching into my life in San Francisco again, despite his wife and three in Lorain, saying, "Hey, I'll bet you know some good ones around here," I cannot count him among the marital successes. (I do count a few. Everyone counts a few. No one counts many.)

Let me tell how the women of thirty got divorced in San Francisco. First there was one who said, "He's boring. He's okay. I want more. I want out." Then another who said: "He drinks a little, but it isn't that. I want to be *me.*" And another who said: "You only live once and I don't want this to be the once." And another: "I don't have to explain to anyone. It's over."

What they were declaring was: Anatomy is not destiny;

choosing destiny is destiny. And they found this freedom good. And they chose. And the choices begat other choices. Good, good, good.

Trouble.

To my wife I said, "These friends of yours are the Four Horsewomen of the Apocalypse, thank God."

But there was a fifth crack-up. Ours.

And then a sixth, seventh, I can't count how many. One woman went off to live with a lover in Los Angeles but then returned to her husband, worn, not happy, "for the sake of the children and why not?" The others didn't leave for a man; they didn't come back for one, either.

They live in groups with other women, sharing the mothering with occasional overnight men visitors. The children tend to cling more seductively to these lovers than do their mothers.

They date again, and wonder how this has happened to them all over again.

They are bemused by their Passages.

They are fulfilling themselves as striving feminists. They have women friends and men friends. They think this is okay, not great. "If it's a nice day," one said, "and I enjoy my coffee, and I can look forward to a warm-hearted man, no particular one, after the kids are in bed, that's okay. It's not the ecstatic life. But it's okay."

"Okay?"

"What we're after is *sensual,* not *sexual.* Pleasure where it happens, not all that greedy devouring."

"Is there a price?"

She shrugged. "Might be. Look at the price that other way —so much misery. So we'll see about this way."

An odd thing about the new fashion for single parenthood, usually the woman who does the nurturing, though sometimes it is a man, is that it reconstitutes the family—except without what defines a family, that system of balanced responsibilities. Women live alone plus child care, or in communes or tribes, or with another single mother, or sometimes with a single father, sharing aspects of child-rearing. It is the family again, with two important legs missing. The urge to some kind of family seems very strong. On the frontiers, showing the power of this impulse, is a fledgling organization here in San Francisco: The Association for the Defense of Lesbian Fathers. These women don't accept the mother's role, but they do accept a parental one. They want to have kids who admire them for strength, wage-earning, world-beating. They may be parodies of ancient history in an androgynous world. They may be sports. They are playing their games, too.

This is a generation of marriage casualties. George Gilder's book, *Naked Nomads*—which many feminists don't like—says that men are the great sufferers. Women can do without men; men only think they can do without women. Doing without means living in hope, hunting, haunting fern bars, being obsessed—that's not doing without, not freedom, not independence.

Now serendipity strikes again. As I wrote the above paragraph, a lovely young dancer knocked at my door. I didn't remember her name, but I had met her as she was moving out (helped carry a guitar, a box of books) a few doors away, a few months ago. I had said then: "Wish I knew you when you lived here." She was moving to Hawaii to be with her sort of true love. Their karma was good. He was an Aries and she . . . So here she is back again, having just walked up Russian Hill, looking for another apartment in the neighborhood.

"What happened?" I asked.

"The guy wasn't there when I was there. He isn't a real man. Who needs it?"

"Right," I said, "wanna have lunch after I write a few more paragraphs on this article?"

"Okay, but I got this funny news, could be a bringdown when I think about it." She had walked up the hill from the public health clinic. They had just finished telling her she was pregnant. She's thinking of having the baby.

I said: "Who's the father?"

"One of three," she said. "I got kind of lonely when my old man wasn't there."

Her father is a wealthy lawyer. He'll help, she said, he'll be the man in her life, there are lots of men for a girl who looks . . . She shrugged modestly.

I raised all the questions about the single mother, including the question about genes if you don't know the father very well. She sighed. It's a question. When she left—tune in again for further news—she had not decided yet whether or not she wanted to go into motherhood just now. But the idea seems natural, she feels good, men like her—"look how you picked up on me right away, you must have felt something," she said.

I felt something. She liked what I felt. But she doesn't really need a man in this world, she thinks, and can't understand how her child will cling to any man in sight as a frazzled single parent learns to be thirty, to be thirty-five, passing the time through a world where karma is not everything.

This carefree dancer might or might not decide to have her baby conceived by that lonely week on Oahu. But someday she will have one, and probably won't be ready to stay with a man till she is past the middle of her life, and there is no way in the world her course can be stayed. The flower revolution has settled in. The karmic kids don't smell of jasmine and ginseng but of diapers and milky burps, like other kids.

At the other end of marriage stands the tradition. In

Mount Clemens, Michigan, a bride is suing her husband for defamation of character because he told friends and family she wasn't a virgin when they married. They adhere to the Sicilian concept of virtue, and there wasn't sufficient blood on the sheets on their wedding night, and the bride is outraged at her groom's outrage. They are still married, but one might infer it is not a happy marriage.

When I separated from my wife, my old-world mother asked: "Are you divorced yet?" Finally I said, "Yes, it's final." "Oh I'm happy for you," she said. "Now you can date."

Everything that ever was in marriage and courting and sexuality still exists. The proportions are different. Things seem freer, but the tightness and convention and religion and societal sanctions are intact. The flower revolution and experimentation and total freedom are also still intact.

While the Sicilian tradition of honorable virginity remains alive in Mount Clemens, Michigan—and also in certain neighborhoods of San Francisco and New York—gay couples are arguing that the next frontier of gay liberation is same-sex marriage, legal and religious. "Why should heterosexual couples get all the esteem, the tax advantages?" asked a gay lawyer here in San Francisco.

"Well, the family unit is designed, it seems, for the protection of children, for the nurturing of children?"

"But doesn't it apply even when there are no children? And don't many couples decide not to have children? And don't many gay couples want to adopt children? What do you mean about marriage?"

Indeed, what do we mean about marriage? The boundaries are shifting in a way to make one seasick. I would boil a cup of coffee at this point, except that I can't bear to walk into my kitchen: too messy. I've let things slide. My cleaning man canceled out this week because he was having a quarrel with his boyfriend.

Is this some kind of countercultural margin we are all living on here? Is it all gay marriage, single parenthood, frantic serial monogamy, open marriage with its attendant closedness, jealousy, colossal rages, frustration, romantic catastrophe? No, of course not. Everyone knows the ancient codgers who have stayed married for fifty years, joyfully following the famous injunction of St.-Exupéry which used to get embroidered on pillows, given to dates at girls' schools, bought on plastic parchment in Old Town to get posted in our cozy nests: Love consists not in spending a lifetime gazing into each other's eyes, but in looking in the same direction. It could have been Kahlil Gibran, too, but it was St.-Exupéry, and the point is: It works for a few.

Linus Pauling, twice a Nobel laureate and now, in his ninth decade, in the forefront of Vitamin C research, has such a deal with his wife. They have been together forever, they love each other forever.

Vera Nabokov, wife of Vladimir, the author of *Lolita*, who died at age near eighty, is another survivor of marriage at the highest level of intellect and achievement.

My own parents celebrated their fiftieth wedding anniversary a few years ago, and there has never been a question of any other solution than their marriage to the problem of loneliness, trust, confidence, sharing, defiance of mortality.

The rich and famous do it, and the nonrich and nonfamous also provide examples of the miracle. But the business which provides this percentage of failure cannot be called a good business. If you could visit a cholera epidemic and only one in five or one in ten would come out unscathed, you might decide not to visit a cholera epidemic. Marriage is something almost everyone visits, and these days it is a factory for the production of grief.

How do I know about Linus Pauling and his wife? Well, a former wife, making a new life away from her former friends, got to know the great scientist and his wife and she told her former husband. Why can't we do the same, live happily, productively, humorously ever afterward? he asked her. Well, because it's a new time . . . a new and serious passage in her life . . . We can be best friends, or some kind of friends—maybe former friends—while she listens to her different drummer, or puts her ear to the ground to catch the thrumming of the hooves of some *parfait cavalier* on his white horse, or just finds a job to do, or joins forces with all the other young women of thirty with a child or two or three, or . . . Wasn't marriage made to surround the kids with care? Well, we have child-care centers now; we live too long to need the protection of mother-wives or father-husbands; we are harboring in our reactionary bosoms an institution which was rigidly defined in a time when everything, religion and sex and science and money and health and travel and every goddamn element—geriatrics and frozen yogurt —which defines civilized life was different.

The institution doesn't yield too well, it doesn't evolve easily. And when it doesn't, the walls tend to crack on the heads of those below. Love is still grand, and the greatest joy. And for most, the end of love, the crack-up of marriage, is still the deepest grief. In the unbalance of it all, most of us remember the grief and panic of severance more than the joy of looking into eyes which promise perfect oceanic union. "Dissolution"—the California term for divorce— really means the dissolution of personality and of the old sense of self.

Assuming survival, the self is put together again and we start looking for another solution. It had better not be repetition of the old hopes. Marriage is like a Baskin-Robbins franchise shop—it changes flavors regularly, but tends to be reassuringly familiar. "My first husband was mean to me—

my second was sweet," a lovely actress told me. "So now I don't know what I want. Maybe a place in Malibu."

Sometimes, with young children who live ten blocks away from me with their mother, I feel like a freeway father, making complicated interchanges involving my former wife and the kids, her friends, my friends, their kids, our kids . . . Is this what we meant, dearest, when we picnicked on Mount Tamalpais and lay looking up at the buzzing, blooming glory of sky and God's trust? Last summer I took my children to Lake Tahoe. There was no woman, no wife to share the duties of a household. We camped out in sleeping bags, buried a pet lizard which died, explored geological layers with old spoons, bought "supplies" instead of food. At the end of the week, happy and skinny, I wanted to write a confession, "I Was a Male Mother." I had fun, I don't feel sorry for myself—but you mean this is what single parents do all the year long? No wonder the women who want their freedom, break their marriages, are then so avid to find a new "living arrangement"—other women, other men, communes, tribes, nervous-breakdown remedies.

Yes, it's hard to raise children, even with child-care centers, buses, playground teams, car pools. Maybe it needs two people in the house, and the question of "dating"—waiting for true love to ring the phone—kind of temporarily settled. When a child cries, and says it's the toy truck that's lost, or the dollhouse which broke, it may be the truck or the dollhouse but forevermore we will not know for sure if the tears are not for the family which is broken. Everybody is very careful with these children. How good of us. But how nice if perhaps it couldn't have remained just one big careless family.

"What did you learn this summer, Ethan?"

"I learned a lizard's eyes fall out when they die and it gets all kind of stiff."

"That's nice. I'm sure your father had fun, too."

In the great wisdom of the time of togetherness, when we believed marriage on its four legs to be as strong, stable, and indestructible as a trusty old inherited dining-room table, we used to tell ourselves wisely during the time of the itch: "The reasons we stay married are more important than the reasons we got married."

Those are powerful reasons.

But it turns out that the reasons to end marriage are more urgent than both. Romance and the deepening of love, stability and the nurturing of history in the form of children and memories, seem to be as naught compared to self-fulfillment, often imagined as Self-Fulfillment. Sure, it can be done within the structure, but—

But it can be done differently without the structure, and what we want is the different. Everyone wants a piece of strange (mistress, lover, adventure with the hippie guitarist or the downtown secretary). Everyone also wants something permanent to carry him through the night, to be the lovers in Dylan Thomas's poem, bodies interlaced, "their arms 'round the griefs of the ages."

Piety used to consist in obedience to the Judeo-Christian family structure—marriage forever and ever, till death, usually in the twenties or early thirties, do us part. Now piety consists in loyalty and obedience to nude therapy, swing club, self-actualizing, I'm-okay-where-are-you?, est, fernbar, singles apartment complex, charter romance, vibrator or rubber dollie adventure, the pursuit of what Will Schutz, author of *Joy* and *More Joy* has called Humpo; that is, the Human Potential Movement. These leisure sports often leave the griefs of the ages impacted in our souls, except perhaps at rare moments of intimacy or contemplative satisfaction. And isn't that comfort and exhilaration, when mortality is defeated and the griefs turned to triumph, what we all seek to draw out of ourselves with the aid of others, spouse, lovers, new spouse, respouse, primaries, satellites, friends?

Here is a list from a book review by Alix Nelson in the *New York Times* of the problems of "the conventional nuclear family unit":

Sexual boredom
Rigid divisions of labor
Stultifying role expectations
Possessiveness
Dependency
Anger
Apathy
Isolation from friends
Loss of freedom and spontaneity
Inability to grow and experiment
Making decisions based on compromise (everybody
   feels trapped and cheated)

and who is to deny that all these straws would break any normal camel's back? The solutions of greater flexibility include (another list):

One-parent households, father or mother in charge
Unwed parenthood
Several women sharing, a female tribe
Communes of men & women sharing tasks, parenthood, & each
   other
Rotating parenthood between mother & father who live apart
Polygamous families . . .

Whoops, there goes another camel's back. The search for both freedom and community, human needs which should not be mutually exclusive but usually are, continues. Some solutions provide adventure, excitement, risk—and no security and kindness. Some solutions provide stability and steadily deepening understanding—and no fun.

Yet love is not dead on this desolation row. Even ended marriages endure in a form which is the enemy of neatness: the children. And as I write this, I think of my eight-year-old daughter. I dreamed of love and holding, of long nights forever, of busy days forever, with one woman who would cherish me equally. I woke from this dream. But nothing, nothing, nothing can remove that child from my heart and, I like to think, until she starts the love round herself, nothing will remove me from hers.

But then, here too, there will be a kind of divorce.

The girl with the three impregnators in Hawaii returned to see me before I finished this essay. "Well, you were right," she said, "my karma said do it."

"Do what?"

"I got the abortion."

Her smile demanded the lame response which I heard falling from my mouth. "Congratulations."

The smile was brilliant and convincing, and the girl is lovely. "I'm looking for some better genes for the father of my child. I thought you might know somebody."

12
Ballad of the Freeway Father

The snow is falling in Detroit, in Cleveland, in Milwaukee, in Boston, all over the mountain-high waves of the Atlantic; the eastern seaboard is socked in; radiators are hissing in Manhattan and a lot of mommies have sinus headaches; and sliding in an avalanche of cold, of cool, of icy, of silent wind and love-starved snow-creatures, a man comes to rest outside a door in suburban someplace. He has ridden a plane from elsewhere to see his children. The plane was sprinkled with the frazzled faces of fathers taking advantage of the school holiday. He has rented a car. He doesn't have gloves or scarf; he came from California.

"Just a minute!" calls the face at the window. He knows that dear face—his former wife. His children are a little late downing their Post Toasties and she wants them to finish a good breakfast to prepare for their arduous day at the motel with their father. His husband-in-law, his successor in the arms of the lady, is still at home and doesn't enjoy his presence on the scene. The snow turns his shoulder white; it crunches underfoot as he turns in a circle, like a trapped buffalo. *When are the damn kids gonna be ready?*

A buzzer sounds. Mercy has come to the Midwest—a compromise between not wanting his presence and a little elemental compassion. He is admitted to the vestibule, and now waits another twenty minutes amid the bone-piercing damp of yesterday's mud-encrusted overshoes. Two children, one with egg on mouth, appear suddenly, with those welcoming words: "What did you bring us? Where are we going? It's not going to be museums again, is it?"

"Say a hi daddy first. Kiss first."

"Hi, daddy. What you bring us? We ate already, so what else we gonna do?"

When they are older, they will be put on planes to visit daddy in his lair. Instead of saying, "What we gonna do?" in Detroit, Milwaukee, Cleveland, Boston, or Manhattan, they can come to California to say it; or wherever daddy is. Daddy is irked by the elimination of special children's fares on airplanes. He flies his missions and then his bombardier children fly theirs, dropping loads of guilt on the overpopulated strategic hamlet of his skull.

As evening falls across the terrace at Enrico's Coffee House in San Francisco, a man lounges there with his date. There is a single rose in the vase on the table. The lady is sipping her ginger ale with four lethal food-additive blood cherries (the waiter likes her). She waits for her *trois petits hamburgers* on sesame bun. They come with a little chili. The man holds her hand across the table. A romantic sizzle of outdoor space heaters; a baroque hum of FM Vivaldi. The lady is calm, lovely, smiling, and six years old.

Twenty years ago, another six-year-old girl is going to the movies on a Saturday afternoon on the east side of Manhattan. It may have been a Danny Kaye film. The father nods at men whose names he doesn't know, but he has seen them at Mayhew's ice cream parlor on Madison Avenue, he has seen them in the lobbies with their children, he recognizes the faces. As the blacks (still called Negroes) had fraternal palm-slapping handshakes, so these tragical, happy-problem fathers should have secret signals, popcorn breath, cholesterol, and candy-stuck salutes. They know each other without knowing each other.

After one marriage I was that father in New York. And now, after another, I am the father in San Francisco.

A scarred veteran of marital wars, here I stand to tell something about what it feels like to be the father of five mother-raised children. I am an expert in Doggy Diner evenings, east side afternoons at the movies, weekend what-do-we-do-now discussions, museum explorations all over this great nation, cross-country get-to-know-each-other tours, existential discussions of whether the generative blood father really understands cavity and allergy problems, waiting-room attendance for the kids to get their cuddlies collected, while the new husband or lover hides in the kitchen; the spurious cool and friendliness of old lovers, forever parents exchanging neutral comments about how well everyone looks. . . . I have spent two generations in the cinder parking lot of the Frosty Freeze. I am the freeway parent of five children by two wives.

Thanks to the miracles of modern medicine, vitamin pills, clean living, a healthy metabolism, and ancestors genetically cursed with long life, I have two daughters in their twenties. I look back on their childhood, which I shared with the help of frequent airplane trips, and feel pleased that I kept the connections alive. It was worth it. They are fine young women, and I count on their visits when I sink into second childhood. (I hope to win the neck-and-neck race between wisdom and senility.)

I now also have another daughter of six, no, seven—the

ages keep clicking away—and twin sons who are five, and am repeating the adventure of fatherhood from a certain distance.

In the first family there was some ex-wifely resentment of my remaining alive and persistent. In the second case, there is friendly cooperation and good fellowship. Having tried both hatred and love, I'm here to say that love is better. Conjugal and marital love might be best, but the mutual trust of old companions and sympathetic parents is better than its opposite.

The statistics about divorce are also the statistics about freeway fatherhood, give or take a few childless unions. One in three marriages ends in divorce. Others end in desertion, for reasons of money or color or religion, where divorce is beyond the ken. So the father is just not there. (For him, the *children* are not there.) In a certain number of cases—let's make up a fraction: $5/17$—the father says, Shucks, it's too much bother, I'm off for the West or Nam or Elsewhere, and I'll call myself Tex or Slim, and let 'em try to find me. . . . He nightmares his children; that's all, if he's not a psychopath. And the kids learn to live with Mommy and Uncle, or Mommy and Nobody, and another pattern of fatherless life is established. Nowadays, of course, it's often women who choose freedom, riding off into the noon, dreaming of romance and freedom and independence and adventure and truth and beauty and no dirty socks to pick up. Look out, America. The unitary family fragments itself in many unsparkling ways.

Some of my fellow freeway fathers are delightful chaps, with deep feelings and nice tricks to play on kiddies and wife. In general, they are decent human beings. Nevertheless, in general, their wives object to their hanging about and make it difficult for them—they stand in the street, in the snow, they get cold shoulder and hot tongue, they feel frozen out by the person who once cuddled them in. It's easier to forget the whole bad deal. Court orders and common garden variety pleading don't soften the heart of an outraged spouse. It hardens the resolution. Dignity unpreserved, gone sour, brings a fine flush of contempt. The freeway father, to establish his authority over his children—I am your father, I know which vitamin pills to take, I can decide a parent's issues—needs a miracle. There aren't as many miracles as there used to be. He tries to make do with stubbornness. Stubborn fatherhood is to natural fatherhood as "The Star-Spangled Banner" is to passionate natural patriotism. He sings like a father, he talks like a father, but it's all just standing around the football stadium, waiting for the real game to begin.

Now let's sample a bit of sociology, although probably our life experiences, all those kids and daddies we know, would be more instructive. An interesting book by the behavioral scientist David Lynn, *The Father: His Role in Child Development,* makes the point that the absent father seems to produce, in these unbalanced single-parent families, a tendency to lowered I.Q., social uncertainty, poor adjustment, lack of popularity, failure to assume leadership, lowered self-esteem, diminished respect for tasks, uneasy sexual identification, poorer physical development, greater delinquency —in other words, every imaginable disadvantage but cauliflower blight. On the other hand, certain signs of creativity are augmented, and it might be that some manifestations of genius, in addition to craziness, come of the child's need to cope with a pattern of quarrelsome parents followed by absent daddy. Dr. Lynn warns against making trouble in the family so you can produce artists and writers, since the odds are that you'll simply produce a macho kid creep or a weepy street whiner. The genius will unearth his own family troubles, whatever he needs, and make himself into Shakespeare (or Hamlet) with what life brings his way. He will discover broccoli rust and *define* it as cauliflower blight.

For those who want to increase their load of guilt, I recommend chapter 15, "The Absent Father." If your quota of uneasiness has not been filled this month, you can find just the tickets here.

Of course, broken families are not another planet from closed ones. In tight or patched-together families games are played, roles fulfilled, expectations and ghosts and fantasies evoked and exorcised. Circulating invisibly about the heads and hearts of everyone in family are the spectors and echoes of the past. I relate to my son as my father related to me, as his grandfather related to his father; or in the opposite way; or in another way—but always *because* we have a history. There is a pattern to be followed or to be violated. There are rules. The difference is the amount of play, and in family, with the united energies of mother and father, authority comes easier. The rules are clearer. There is some confidence of unity.

In the awful time of chagrin, when his nightmare puts him in a lonely room with no one, in a lonely house with nobody, in a routine of responsibilities without joy, the freeway father may even doubt that his children are really his children —how does he know he really conceived them, when his wife has demonstrated that she doesn't need him, he is not unique, her life is elsewhere? And these shy strange brats whom he courts so lumberingly—what mad pride makes him assume they are blood of his blood, bone of his bone?

Reassertion of his pride and pleasure in fatherhood is difficult when the chief routine is the writing of the monthly child-support check and the scheduling of "visitations"—a legal term which suggests sudden mystical descent by airy spirits.

Delicacy and Nagging are the two extremes of freeway fatherhood etiquette.

Delicacy: everyone is careful, as if we are made of moral china, not to break the spirit of precarious togetherness. One takes tea with one's children, white gloves spotless. "What do you want to do?" "I don't know, what do you want to do, daddy?" This Marty-esque dialogue ends in the aforesaid horrid museum treks, ice cream sorties, condolence calls to other single parents—a prolonged wake over the corpse of togetherness. Nothing is said. All is Thank you, Please, and You're welcome. Anything you like, dear. We all live in a yellow submarine—or would you prefer it to be beige?

Nagging: ah, that is worse; certainly painfilled—it expresses what we really feel! *Don't!* is the favorite word, as in: Don't eat with your fingers, don't spill that, don't jump on the couch, don't do whatever you're doing which your don't-be-a-full-time-dad disapproves of. He is loading on you all the dump truck of disapproval, hope, dream, sour rearrangement. And it's a two-way street, of course. Very soon the precious angel becomes a brat, saying to Dad: Don't brush your hair like that, are you trying to hide you're bald? Don't keep taking us to the same old places, don't visit that woman with us (we *hate* her!), especially don't touch her when you think we're not looking. Do we all live in a yellow submarine? But we don't *like* yellow submarines. How about yellow depth charges?

Most often, a little duet of Delicacy and Nagging ensues, alternative melodies played out during the intense periods of Visitation. Moral barriers of manner and etiquette are erected, of revenge and caring, of regret. Over the years, the upfront anger fills more of the need for genuine family connection than the eighteenth-century gavotte of politeness. At least there is passion. There may be tears. If the last frontier is marriage-sex-family-divorce, we are awake in the firing line. The polite option is comparable to dying in your sleep, without the option of speaking a last word to the survivors. Professor Corey's argument applies: "I believe in hatred, because without hatred there is no joy in revenge." A spunball confusion of emotions rolls down the pike. New barriers, new freedoms.

The freeway father learns to bear it in mind that people are unpredictable, i.e., difficult to fathom, i.e., difficult to live with. Isn't that why he lives alone? *She* is unfathomable? *He* is difficult? As wives, so children. As Kissinger, so Brezhnev. The freeway father has a good place in line at the reality soup kitchen. One thing he can predict is that penetrating kid war cry: "Daddy! I want—"

Ice cream, a movie, a new pair of jeans, a peepee, an answer to a knock-knock riddle, nothing, and something daddy can't give—steady protection against the world's evil weathers.

Choose one or several of the above. Except for the latter; on that, write an essay worth eighteen years of attention and care. The balanced unitary family has given the world plenty of mass murderers, schizophrenics, paralyzed neurotics, ordinary downer-people, and yet it's the way we persist in seeing proper human affections. A single log won't burn in the fireplace; to be properly ignited, it needs air space and another log nearby (some kindling will do in a pinch). The kids nestling near the anxious body of the spousal-support ex-bride feel that lack of air, that lack of another log. They are deprived. They are angry.

Daddy comes back to visit his children during Visitation and hears them singing, Please stay with us, please stay, we need you, daddy. *I can't.* Then hit the road, Jack, and don't you come back no more, no more, no more.

Hatred and love, need and demand, nightmares of trust betrayed, these contradictions fly like phlegm and spittle through the abstract outer space of child support.

Another of the problems of the freeway father is what happens when he happens to have friends. The friends say: "Come visit us, bring the kids."

He does so.

Then he has a woman friend and the friends say: "Good. How nice and healthy for you. Come visit us with the kids and with *her*."

(Whisper, whisper. He dumped his wife for a younger creature.)

I remember showing up with my two adolescent daughters and my woman companion and my old buddy said: "Ah! Here he comes with his three children."

Friends, particularly married friends, sometimes imagine all the great sex, great fun, great freedom the new bachelor has. Sometimes they are right. And sometimes, although they are right about the delicious warm sex, the delicious warm cuddling with lonely children, the avidness of moments of miracle, these moments are still not something the freeway father would not exchange for regular breakfasts with his kids, regular bedtimes with his kids, regular evenings with a wife who is also the mother of those kids. He would turn in the champagne and gypsy violins for a reprise of beer at the kitchen table.

His woman friend says: "Look, they're your problem, you take care of them." (That's if she is that luminous teenybopper which the old buddy envies.) Or, if she is the nursie lady who seeks to rescue shipwrecked fathers after their marital wars: "Poor baby, I'll do it for you."

But who wants to travel with a nursie? Even for the sake of the kids? I don't. No more than the ex-wife wants to substitute Mr. Wilfred Gooduncle with his tolerant nature for her vision of Sir Anthony Stunning, burning-eyed and peculiar.

Now let us proceed to a delicate topic, one of the few remaining undisputed negatives of moral behavior. A general taboo always stands for a general desire. It is forbidden nearly everywhere to enjoy one's own children carnally, whether heterosexually or homosexually, and even with consent of all parties, and even if promises are kept and the proper mating ceremonies performed. No, *no,* Mummy and Daddy and Dick and Jane.

A new dimension is added to the incest taboo by the broken family. In normal togetherness (remember the fifties?) morning and evening cuddles, another fond parent looking on, kept the bodies legally warm and thrumming. The single stick in the fireplace won't burn; we know that. The more sticks, the better. There is continual household touching. It is permitted; it is encouraged; daddy and mummy belong together, so this other stuff is just a part of their bonding.

But in a broken family, the daddy visits like a swain, and the cuddling is replaced by passionate embraces of greeting and farewell. Fantasy extrapolates. What does all this mean?

Once I visited a psychoanalyst friend and waited for him while he took his well-paid hour with a patient. The patient drove up in a red Alfa-Romeo, she was blonde and delicious and had a jaunty stride, she looked like a soap and cigarette advertisement, not anything that required Valium or pity. I fell in love. He wouldn't introduce me.

Later I asked for news of her. The good doctor told me that, to begin with, she was a successful young model, had inherited money, and had slept with her father through high school and college. "Slept with her father?" I repeated dumbly. He made a Detroit smallboy gesture of finger jabbing through circled other fingers. I whistled. "Man, she does have problems," I said.

"Well, the main problem is her mother," said my friend, sucking on his pipe. "You see, she knows her father loves her. She's not so sure about her mother."

I stammered: Incest, guilt, shame, invocations of the Bible, the Judeo-Christian ethic, the passion of Islam, the caution of Melanesia and the Eskimos—it's forbidden!

"Ah, my friend. About her father she *knows*," he said.

13
"The Therapist Will See You Now, Big Boy" (Deep Carpet: The Tragic Bust of the Golden Gate Foundation)

Eighteen San Francisco vice squad heroes raid a Victorian house on Bush Street in San Francisco, arresting six women and one black male on the charge of prostitution. Hundreds and hundreds of man-hours went into this police triumph. Yet Kitty Desmond, Executive Planning Director, appeared in newspapers proud and smiling, alert, to declare that the "Golden Gate Foundation, Research and Development"—plaque on the door—was only performing a psycho-medical service. That bordello atmosphere was just for mood and fun; the women are therapists, surrogates, and fill out forms to prove it. The cops say they were only organizing vice a little better. They were helping along the storied criminal weapon, "feminine charm," with a little cunning modern refinement, recording what the johns like best.

The case accumulated lawyers, briefs, publicity. Indignation, the bedrock quality of radical politics, fueled both sides. Everyone expected history to be made. These fuckers are not whores; yet these sexual partners received no prescriptions from doctors. It's a paradox which needs explanations.

Often a man relieved by a lady of the tensions of modern life-style, those nagging inferiorities which anyone but a brute tends to suffer from time to time, will give a little gift of cash to the agent of transference from psychic pain through lust to a feeling of peace and tastefully unclogged prostate. What psychiatrist or family doctor can do the same? This is a healing art which Kitty, Shirley, Randy, Bonnie, Sandy, and so many unsung others perform. Let us now sing them. These are therapists and surrogates with hearts of gold. It's true. If you feel good, and you think it's nice, and there is no painful urination the next day, it is superbly real and true and beautiful. A fellow might like to make a little cash contribution for the cause of his own well-being, and so much the better if it furthers the work of the Foundation. It costs no more than some untrustworthy call girl.

Bernard Apfelbaum, director of the Berkeley Sex Therapy group, which does professional work on sexual problems, said Kitty's outfit is not *professional.* But Michael Metzker, a former D.A. who was one of the battery of defense attorneys, said the scientific professional establishment is, in contemporary legal jargon, just "covering their asses." Victimless crime infringes on the prerogatives and reputations of the psychiatric establishment. Captain Gerald Shaughnessy, known as The Reverend Captain, reputedly seized three thousand documents in the raid. The American Civil Liberties Union was called in. Galileo, too, had trouble with the cops.

One of the arresting officers observed that much "bulk laundry was regularly carried inside"—a sure proof that this was a House. Well, no one denies they had a use for large quantities of bulk laundry. Kitty lived there, too, and liked a tidy atmosphere.

While they awaited trial, the ladies brooded. The tangerine lights, the incense, the fireplaces, the fine-tradition elegance and gentility were enough to make strong men weep with regret for this waste of youth and energy in legal hassles. A certain number of strong men came around to weep at the iron gates on Bush Street.

And now let's visit cozy Kitty Desmond, her man, and her ladies. . . .

This is one of those really rotten male fantasies I am living out. I would be having dinner with the madam and the entire servicing staff of the most distinguished whorehouse in San Francisco, if this were a whorehouse. I am surrounded by Victorian luxury, carpets so deep you get the staggers as you hike around the house, and really clean, medically-approved, highly trained and educated young women.

Of course, the times and history demand a new way of seeing. These women of the female persuasion are professional ladies. Although busted on charges of procuring and servicing, they are performing a social service, with all their in-and-out, water sports, discipline, French and Arabian and for all I know Canadian activities designed to increase the world's stock of knowledge.

In this time of recession, I sent out to the Flying Chinese Chicken for dinner. I also provided a distinguished collection of genuine Napa Valley wines, including Gallo Red and Foremost White.

The Golden Gate Foundation consists of sexual therapists, sexual facilitators, sexual surrogates, and good food and drink in a funky, elegant Victorian mansion with gas grate hissing like in an old Charles Laughton film (Vincent Price? Bela Lugosi?); not just another bunch of whores and pimps; get that clear right at the start. They did sex labor and research on clients, customers, subjects, not johns, until the assiduous raiders of The Reverend Captain Shaughnessy's San Francisco vice squad stampeded in (some of their own men had their shorts around their ankles at the time) and handcuffed them and messed up their drawers and looked in their Chinese boxes and other games for dope and made a big deal of it. Now a staff of sixteen lawyers is working to save the Golden Gate Foundation from prison terms. A couple more are working on other angles. Over twenty lawyers are involved in trying to put the Golden Gate Foundation back on its feet so that Kitty Desmond, chief Sexual Facilitator and Therapist, can get on with her research.

One damp and foggy July evening, there I was enjoying a take-out dinner of Chinese goodies with Kitty herself, plus Shirley, very young sexual surrogate, she's twenty; Randy, mature sexual surrogate, graduate student out of five or six colleges and universities, doing her groundbreaking thesis on Incestuous Pedophilia, soft Southern accent, she's thirty-one; plus Michael Harris, Kitty's special friend, lean, handsome, articulate, indignant, black, former owner of a chain of boutiques (we pronounce it bo-tique out here), who helped to decorate the house and was, naturally, accused of being a pimp. He's not. He's just Kitty's good friend and helper and a scholar of Masters & Johnson, Kinsey, and Wilhelm Reich, and getting onto this new field of sexual therapy before it's taken over by General Mills or the Mafia. There's still room here for the small innovative operator—sort of like Grove Press attacking Random House with Beckett and Burroughs and the *Evergreen Review.*

"Did you get your 501 C-3 Certificate?" a shrewd voice asked Kitty.

I had also invited a friend to this evening dinner conference, this takeout repast, one of my personal staff of lawyers, Rubin Glickman.

"Wah?" asked Kitty.

"The 501 C-3 Certificate," Rubin said, "makes you a non-profit foundation so the johns can contribute money and get a tax deduction."

Not yet. They hadn't been operating a year before they got busted. Six women and Kitty makes seven, plus Michael, makes eight. But they're planning to open again soon, pending legal disposition. "We're going to do sensitivity training until our legal business is settled," Kitty said.

"We did low-profile fucking like Masters and Johnson. We were helping out men with premature ejaculation problems, sadism problems, water sport problems, exhibitionism and voyeurism problems, oh"—a wave of the hand which included so many memories—"we knew we were under surveillance. If we thought we were illegal, we'd have closed up." The sign right outside the door on Bush Street said, Golden Gate Foundation. They were proud.

"Our business was emotional therapy research. Sexual dysfunction. Lots of our clients are happily married men who just needed a little help, a helping hand, a listening ear," Michael said.

"The cops," Kitty interrupted bitterly, "classified the business as 'Other.'"

"They never heard of Masters and Johnson."

"Our institute would teach expansion of your sexual functions, like a religious trip. We kept complete records on our clients, including preference and type. Would we do that if we weren't a research operation? Does the Mafia bother with such crap? Does this place look like it was decorated by the Mafia?" Randy asked.

"We sanded it down ourselves," said Michael. "We got down to the original wood. It's pretty now."

"It's beautiful."

"The landlord loves us. He never had a tenant like us."

We sipped wine and enjoyed the hissing grate and Randy and Shirley and Kitty and Michael told me about their families and their pre-bust past. Artists, engineers, cops, and alcoholics in their families, just like everybody else. Nice smart friendly girls, and now they're being hassled. They can't lead decent ordinary lives like anybody else without some undercover cop trying to pick them up on some rinkydink charge of soliciting. Randy wants to get on with her thesis—she knows five girls personally who made it with their dads, and are somewhat marked for life—but naturally all this legal and occupational harassment makes it hard to concentrate on phrase-phrase, paragraph-paragraph, footnote-footnote. Sometimes in San Francisco it seems easier just to drift and not be an innovator.

"Per se," Kitty remarked, "there's not much difference between sex therapy and high-level prostitution as such." She's a former nurse, with a good education in science, and she is aware of distinctions. "When we interviewed college girls for surrogates, we found they often didn't have the slightest understanding. A Master's doesn't qualify you to be a warm and wonderful sex surrogate."

This last comment is one to which many of us in higher education can say Amen and Per Se.

"When we interviewed college girls, like I say, we judged them on neatness, togetherness"—togetherness counts—"and explained how we do emotional therapy research."

"We break men down," said Randy, "into nine sexual types—friend, adventurer, opportunist, guardian, promoter, slave, lover, child—"

"Vice squad is the tenth," said Shirley, and everyone laughed.

Rubin was furiously taking notes, too. When I interviewed Bobby Riggs, all I asked Rubin to do was be my doubles partner when we played tennis. What was he taking so many notes for? Did he plan to send me a bill? Didn't this wine and Chinese takeout and the good company suffice?

"We filled out forms on every client," said Randy. "Fantasies? Excessive fondling? Masturbatory activity? Basic family situation?"

"That type of research rap," somebody said.

"And we never accepted money for the activities engaged in," Kitty said. "Like a doctor, it was for time spent."

"Many came just to talk," Michael said, stretching out his long legs. "Especially during the stock market doldrums, rap rap rap. The public was *sad,* man. They wanted to open up, lay it out. They cried."

"Often they wouldn't talk in front of Michael when he was bartending."

I could see that: some paunchy, flab-gilled, wife-depressed, margin-haunted stockbroker sees this handsome brown dude, just stepping so easy with himself around the girls, and he isn't going to want to open up and cry those sweet, soft, relieving tears.

"So I left off bartending and my basic function went into research," Michael said.

We all—plus the elegant ghosts of Basil Rathbone—stared into the fire. The egg roll debris was demolished. A few grains of rice speckled the thick, worn, unthreatening carpeting. Rubin Glickman tapped his nose. Was he going to cry, too, like so many men in this parlor? No; just meditating.

"Women can do things on their own," Kitty stated, "good things. Michael put out energy, too." I had the impression that Kitty and Michael were close friends, old friends; she used to manage one of his chain of bo-tiques in Sausalito. "We here at the Golden Gate Foundation are not just 'a houseful of staunch feminists' "—this sounded like a quotation from someplace—"no, we're *women.*"

Right on.

"We're over eighteen, we're not girls or whores like those cops keep trying to say, we're women. Our customers are not johns. They are visitors. They are clients."

Michael and Kitty both look a little leaner than easy sleep gives—that extra edge of stylish leanness which comes from anxiety and being out on bail. "When we had our fund-raising parties," Michael said bitterly, "the cops said we invited people to contribute to keep their names out of the papers. What bullshit."

"With all the goodies and freebies, we barely broke even on the fund-raising parties," said Kitty.

Sixteen or twenty lawyers is a lot of expenses, even if they are deferring their bills, because they are a staff of the finest young idealistic criminal lawyers in San Francisco, including four or five staunchly feminist women lawyers. Margo St. James, founder and guru-person of Coyote, the Whore's Affinity Group (a union would be illegal), helped to mobilize the community. Even though the Foundation was not a brothel, some of the girls played on her softball team and she came through immediately. Just call someone a whore, even if she's not, and Margo will rush to the defense. (Margo likes cops personally, just hates what they do. Inside, in their hearts of hearts, they're people, too, just like most other folks you meet.)

In the meantime, worldwide, the Golden Gate Foundation is fighting that bordello image the media and the cops insist on giving them. Who says a non-Mafia research foundation can't have plush carpeting, chandeliers, waterbeds, discreet indirect lighting, a few sexy French postcards on the walls? "Listen, we don't even have central heating," Michael said. "Wouldn't a bordello have central heating for those dampish evenings?"

Just like a little research foundation myself, I took a lot of notes and history and could now tell how Michael got out of the chain of bo-tiques in Sausalito and read those books by Miss J., you know, lick the whipped cream off your lover's body—that late sixties kind of groovy shtick. He thought of this new frontier, sex, which isn't tied up like the oil or the automobile business. Remember how Tucker got fucked? Better get into this thing fast. So he and Kitty rented, decorated, planned, bought their three by five research cards, and collected a staff.

Randy remarked, "I was overqualified to be a sex surrogate. I was more like a therapist."

But Kitty was the chief therapist around here. It was her idea, hers and Michael's.

"Anyway, I'm going to do my Master's on Incest Pedophilia. Hardly anyone's done it." By this time you probably realize this is Randy talking again. She has this sweet small Southern voice. I remarked about the affinity with Faulknerian themes in the concerns of this thirty-one-year-old, lovely, and clean surrogate. "The Southern just doesn't have enough sense not to admit it." We were talking about her thesis. "The Northern, four out of five, does it but denies it. It's ironic," said Randy, smiling. "The daddy who is trying to protect you is *doing* it."

We slipped off the subject of incest pedophilia. Everyone has his little hobbies. Me, I like philosophy, tennis, haikus. But we had to stick to business around here. Rubin's time is valuable, too.

Kitty remembered one of the funny little local-color things that happened at a fund-raising party after the bust. An undercover cop kept offering twenty-five dollars to the girls to go upstairs with him. "So I explained a lot about therapy. I talked and talked. Finally he cried. He denied he was a cop, but he cried and said nobody believed him. I finally told him to get out, and he said, If I give you twenty-five, will you go upstairs with me? Still crying because I said he looked so much like a cop."

And then what?

"He got into the plainest-looking Ford you ever saw and drove off, still crying and lying in his teeth."

Kitty feels the clients committed the crime, too, if the cops insist it isn't research; and if researchers into conduct get set on by the law, the johns will have to suffer, too. This theory that they are just "victims of feminine charms" is for the birds. "We're basically sympathetic to our clients," she said ominously, "but."

Michael is sore about being taken for a pimp just because he's black. "Everyone involved should share the heat, not just the girls and one black male." The women too are indignant. These are scientific research foundation-type personnel. "Sure we dress pretty, flimsy, see-through, eye shadow. But we're scientists, like the girl next door."

Despite their irritation with the police action, they make distinctions among cops. "This one guy who had intercourse and fellatio, he arrested us, but he had a scintilla of human feeling. He said, *Don't call them whores,* when his buddy handcuffed us."

"We never denied that there was sexual activity in the Golden Gate Foundation. The cops did it too," Michael explained. "We filled out the sheets on their activity afterwards—premature ejaculations, them guys. We want the public to hear our story."

Vice squad duty is a favorite in police forces everywhere. It's safe, and it has charm. It seems that sometimes you get laid, too. Shirley was making it with another girl at a cop's request, while he knelt at the foot of the bed and masturbated, which was his thing. So she explained. She was sincere about everything, and did as he asked, not faking, because otherwise she would giggle, crack up.

"Men are never whores!" Michael cried. "They can do it with fifty girls and they're not whores. A girl gets to be a whore."

The unfairness of it all lay heavily over the remainder of the Chinese food. Someone remarked about "approach-avoidance" behavior in men and I neglected to ask for explanations. Kitty was saying they'll treat women, too, when they reopen to do sensitivity training. Michael was telling about how he ran the Consumer Fraud Department at San Francisco Consumer Action when he completed his initial studies in sexuality and car business rip-offs.

"This is not a house," Kitty said, "it's my home. I've got to support it."

"Plus it's a secondary education facility," said Michael.

Shirley's father is a police officer.

Randy's father is an engineer. Her mother is a painter.

Kitty was a nurse; her mother is a registered nurse.

None of them get off on being called criminals. "It's an identity problem," Kitty says. "I don't think of myself like that. So we're going to fight all the way."

Sometimes, as I poured through the documentation in the house on Bush Street, and the long San Francisco afternoons passed in careful research, and the girls made me little snacks as low blood sugar overtook me (nothing elaborate), I would leave the scrapbooks and the files to browse in the library near the hissing grate, among such works as *Super Horoscope's Compatability Guide,* which tells how to make astrology really work for you in love, health, and career, "416 fact-filled pages." Even therapists and surrogates are not perfect, I realized, and take counsel and aid where they can.

Leo, the resident large dog, has obscure dreamy troubles, and as I make notes, occasionally licks my shoes and then weeps. I whisper to him: "The fault, dear Brutus, is not in the stars, but in ourselves. . . ."

He stops whimpering and sleeps by the fire. I wonder if a plain panel truck parked outside is monitoring my conversations with the dog.

Some girls whose interest in macrame and Tarot peaked last year have this year found a new hobby: Money. Selling what God gave them, juice and beauty and grace, seemed to be in the cards. They are offering it for rent, and sliding through on wings of science and research.

There might be another side to the Golden Gate Foundation, so I visited Debbie on her houseboat in Sausalito. She is opulent, pretty, young, well educated, with one of those fresh, freckled Irish faces, and worked briefly as one of Kitty's surrogates. Now she travels her mane of tawny hair to an upfront, righteous, no-research, $100-a-session house, and prefers it much better. Although she has a good education—university and art school—she didn't like having to write a mini term paper for each john. "Man, I had to fill out the sheets before I was paid."

"You don't mind being a whore rather than a surrogate?"

"I like to handle the seventy-year-old gentlemen—some of them come three times a night, and I'm sitting on some thirty-year-old dudes who can't do that. Listen, I make sure they get their toes licked. I take it seriously. Most of the time, for $100, I come with them. To me it's a good energy exchange. Each new man is a good study, and it's noble to understand him. I deepthroat—a talent I discovered with a man who said I had a nice singing voice."

"If he's old and ugly—"

"That's a barrier, so I make sure I get through that barrier and he sees Buddha anyway."

Debbie's style is that of the Marin County hip wharf rat.

Her houseboat is filled with books, paintings, and unfinished carpentry. A friend is carving a stairway and stool for the tub. Her sleeping ledge also houses a couple of white cats. Health foods. Honey. A little Kahlua for fun. Some girls would diet at her weight, but she's so friendly, everybody likes her as she is. She seems easy with her body and likes to get off.

She continued to edge into my question about the disagreeable or bad-smelling client. "I get into archetypal energies if he's disgusting. He's a prince, a god, a shepherd on a rock in a meadow. A putoff can be almost more enjoyable. I'm a landlady and I own property back east, so I can make my own choice of what I want to do."

"Do you need to make money this way?"

"There's something called the Hooker's Hook—it means I get a better orgasm when they pay me. The money makes it intense and clear. For example, I have a friend I used to freebie. He used to run his psychological racket against womankind. Now he pays—and he cooks dinner, treats me like a precious object, a princess, and we have a beautiful time. He benefits from the Hooker's Hook, too."

She used to live in a houseboat called "The Clit." That separated the wheat from the chaff among her friends. Now she is constantly improving her new houseboat, using the proceeds—a 60-40 split with the madam—she earns working a few days a week. How would she describe herself as a person?

"I've got good breasts, educated, financially independent, a property owner, an heiress"—her father died when she was sixteen—"an I.Q. of 170, a gourmet cook, writes and paints, songs mostly, and recently I learned I can deep throat. I went to a private girls' school, too. I'm twenty-eight. I sew my own clothing. I made that wooden wall. I'm into carpentry, too. Somebody ripped off all my Bob Dylan records."

Whoring is uncomplicated for her, she says. She is taking her time, waiting for the energy to get together. Kitty's institution was too much like school. Now she can relax. When she's not working, she is making a pillow for her sister, who is about to get married—mountains, stars, sky, and the cutest little felt Indians, all sewed on a nice big foam pillow.

Debbie, retired from sex therapy at Kitty's, declared a nearly Churchillian credo, a war against peace: "I make victory as good as defeat, and failure impossible by changing the rules. There is no failure here."

"You have sure had a good college education," I said. "Personally, I enjoy a good paradox now and then."

"If a guy wants love and rapture, I give it to him. I don't care if he's short of pleasure."

"Ma'm?"

"I mean," she explained painstakingly to a lover of paradox, "I mean premature ejaculation's okay with me."

"You tell him that?"

"I do." She blessed me with her smile. "Which means it surprises him by not happening. Another cure, buster!"

The Sausalito sun was shining above the intimate nest of houseboats in Richardson Bay. What Grover Sales calls "the Bargeoisie" was taking the air, the light, the times. Debbie and I took a box lunch with avocado and sprouts, fruit salad, healthy things from the Brown Bag in San Francisco. It's a good time to hear of inevitable cure-by-definition of the ancient problem of premature ejaculation.

"Good, good," said Debbie, a few sprouts wriggly and pale in the corner of her mouth.

Although Debbie sounded perfectly healthy, our afternoon of sun and sea on her houseboat didn't reveal the mystery. What is life, what is woman, what is Debbie? Perhaps there was another side to her—a complication there someplace. Once she turned down this Sufi, about forty-five, black, great-looking dude, but all he wanted was to seduce her. Why? During a period as a child, her favorite toy was a dead mouse she carried around in a handkerchief. Why? (A neighbor blew the whistle on her.) Sex for Debbie is a mystical oceanic trip, a closeness, and the money? The Hooker's Hook helps to make it perfect and beautiful—yet she is unearthly and mystical in her explanations. From a poem about orgasm by this high-I.Q. lady: *He lay there like a kind of fine silk thread* . . . .

What does Kitty Desmond think of her? Kitty thinks she's not neat and together, she's lazy despite all her activities, she should get her nails done.

In the ease of the afternoon, as the sun moved down over Richardson Bay, I dared to ask whether she would have gone into this line of endeavor if her father had lived.

"My dead father?" Debbie inquired. "We're in tight communication in the spirit world. He's perfectly glad I deep-throated one of his old pals."

The semantic shift to "sex therapist" has made all the difference in the world to a few well-educated, slightly bored, slightly greedy young women. They can turn some tricks for the science of it. And furnish their homes a little more nicely in the bargain. And they are more honest than the girls who constantly run the birthday scam on prosperous men who retain that boyish fix on love.

One wealthy friend of mine, call him Sheldon, complains that he never meets a girl whose birthday isn't next Tuesday. Then after he gives her the birthday present, the relationship seems to peak. He was doing a reprise with one of these urban make-out women after a six-month hiatus, and as we sat there on the terrace of Enrico's Coffee House, I asked her, "Hey, Patsy, what's your sign and when's your birthday?"

"June sixth," she whispered modestly.

"Aw," Sheldon said, "last time we knew each other your birthday was in March. Aw, gee, Patsy."

She didn't even blush. Her fingers were chilly. They needed to be warmed by a bauble.

Some of these girls, it seems, slip into straight talk after awhile. They get tired of lisping "birthday" or "sex therapist" and snap out the ringing words, "I'm a whore."

"What?"

"But I don't have a pimp! I work for myself! I'm a woman and I'm proud and I sell my body."

Margo St. James, deep theoretician, has put it succinctly. The streets must be made safe for walking.

I am sitting in Kitty's kitchen one afternoon, and she is wondering if it's time to do her nails again, and waiting for a call from a lawyer, and feeding me strawberry shortcake, and we are putting our minds to the many problems faced by the Golden Gate Foundation, Research and Development. As she frequently does, forced by events, Kitty is thinking. It's all right to be a crusader, but you've got to get your theory together, too.

Kitty is looking for the word, the right word. "Therapy-for-money," she says. That's not quite it. But she recognizes after all the jabber that what she is doing is not really normal okay medical scientific research & treatment. Not quite. Yet it's not prostitution, either, unless you call dating, marriage, and habitual submission forms of prostitution. "We're inventing something in between," she says. "The best elements of both. We treat dysfunction. We indulge fantasy. How many people go home happy from a marriage? People are lonely in this world. *We assist.*"

Ah, Kitty, but that's not yet enough. You're a nurse and sweet tempered and you do a lot of good, and you're a fighting innovator, too; but we need something more to explain your special role in the world. I think of W. H. Auden's definition of poetry—that which comes from the heart and creates order.

How hard it is to set aside
Terror, concupiscence and pride
Learn who and where and how we are
The children of a modest star—

My friend Rubin and Leo the Dog and all the traffic at the Golden Gate Foundation and myself, too, are seeking to put concupiscence at bay, renew pride, and kill some time on this cold planet. We seek oceanic waves of unity, at-oneness, answers to our mortal sadness, but can be satisfied with pleasure for a time. Nice work if you can get it. Like female genies out of a bottle, the women of the Golden Gate Foundation ask what is your desire, what is your sadness, what is your pleasure.

Oh, it *is?*

And then they hasten to do it . . . *very well.*

Feels like a remedy and cure to almost anyone who goes through it. This is victimless pleasure. The cows are eating the violins and the reverend vice officers are seeking to close down the tingle, confiscate the K-Y jelly. Kitty Desmond, imperfect ideologue, has joined the battle. She will continue to fight, trying to keep the Golden Gate Foundation of San Francisco tidy, cozy, and together.

14
Their Karma Runs over His Dogma (A Sad Story of Sex in San Francisco)

His face was swollen and bandaged. The eyes were bright and alert. Some sort of clever device kept the jaw together. The eyes were emitting sparks of joy in life. Little droplets of blood stained the bindings and bandages. His face was happy through the prosthesis and wires.

"What happened, Virgil?" I asked my neighbor, the Jungian therapist.

"Well, friend, it's so easy to explain, so hard to understand. But if you happen to be a person like me, you shouldn't do your drinking in rough Samoan bars. That's the motto my anima has picked up. Samoan karma and my true gay ways a happy blend do not make."

"Virgil, you're a smart man—"

"Nevertheless I have these fringey emotions I still have to work out," he said. "I know, don't tell me, I know, and thanks a bunch for the neighborly concern. Wanna borrow a cup of gore?"

We in San Francisco live among a population which seems to be shading its sexuality in a series of volcanic eruptions and geologic shifts. It's earthquake time, and the cool gray city is very much concerned with the permutations of love, love, love. Gone today, it will be here tomorrow. In this searchingly optimistic enterprise, San Francisco is perhaps only different in reputation and fanatic zeal from most other places in the U. S., including my stolid, ethnic, bombed-out native place, Cleveland. But we can't pretend that San Francisco really is Cleveland. The changes in sexuality, the obvious play given this instinct, are not so evident and public elsewhere. It's a consumer product which requires very little credit or investment other than the entire soul's commitment. Perhaps for this reason, a renewed commitment to lust seems to be one of the ways people spend their energies in the emerging 1980s. Lust may not redeem, but in a climate of hospitality, espresso, and fern, it tends to console.

As consolation, of course, erotic adventure requires increasing dosages and decoration to retain its effectiveness. San Francisco is a leader in the field of indoor and outdoor, standing and running Olympic sex competition. On my block, for example, a young executive changed from heterosexual Don Juan to transvestite homosexual to slim, long-limbed transsexual in the dozen years we've been neighbors. During the late sixties lovely miniskirted English birds and American flower children visited his house for tea; then boys; and now it's other gawkily feminine creatures like him/herself.

I've learned to be accepting of all my neighbors. I only inquired of Virgil whether he had any conclusions to draw from his facial experience in the Samoan bar.

"It taught me not to do my drinking in such places," he said with the crisp Oxbridge accent that comes over him when his feelings and his body are satisfactorily hurt.

A Sad Story of Sex in San Francisco

"Does that mean you're not going to do it anymore?"

He smiled and shrugged. "Only when I am so inclined," he said.

Besides Virgil, there are other willful, original souls on my block, doing their slanty best to survive in what Charles Dickens called a naughty world.

Late one night, during a rare sudden shower, I saw a man in jockey shorts at his opened door, dramatically smoking and puffing his cigarette out into the storm, starring in a movie of his own devising; he also extended out into the rain an erection of his own devising.

A neighbor lady, noting some of the things we all note about the times, dumped her straight-arrow husband in order to engage in the hobby of bisexuality. "Androgyny is the goal," she informed me. "I don't necessarily prefer men to women, and I don't necessarily prefer women to men, either. What I prefer is reaching my goal, whatever that might be."

"Is it sex on your mind?" I asked. "Pardon me, but it seems this idea of sex should keep you very busy, and yet my sense of you is more of a bemused person—"

"Your sense of me is right on," she said. "I'm an idealist. No, I don't think much about sex. What is sex, after all? Just doing it. No, I think about my course of action, my existential necessity, my karma, my. . . . Where are you going, Herb? Are you late for some uptight appointment in the workaday world which you are still so bound and tied to? Would you like to meet my new friend, the hot handsome hung hunky horny farmer, he plows, he has a dungeon in his cellar, man?"

She had inherited money. She was a sorority girl at Stanford in a time when sororities were falling away from the American educational style. She still looks like a girl, not a woman. She is cute and, I think, as innocent as a child. And yet here she is, trying for something new, pious, and bizarre.

So Virgil, the neighborhood Jungian, is not too far from the folkways of this time and place. He too observed me. "I notice," he said, "being your neighbor and all, you're into a sexuality trip with ladies. But what I don't notice is whether your *sensuality* trip is going okay, friend. *Is it?*"

"I don't think you're meant to notice, Virgil," I said, "but thanks for the concern."

"What are neighbors for?" he asked. "One good confession deserves another. Since you notice my wounds are healing, though my face will always bear these scars. Sort of like Heidelberg dueling scars, I like to think of them, even if they come from brutal action in a Samoan drinking establishment. Later on I'll treat myself to an eyebag-wipeout, plus maybe a little skin abrasion to get rid of that old acne stuff —am I right?"

"Must be," I said.

All this is not about sex, I've begun to understand, but about behavior—how we live now. How we try to survive. How we make out. The people experimenting on themselves are stationed here in San Francisco and trying not merely to snatch the ticket from the automatic dispenser. They're trying to find their very own parking places and bumping into everyone else trying to do the same. They want to be original and they want to be satisfied. Satisfaction no longer comes from a good smoke.

"You try to see clear," the neighbor lady—the one who was "into androgyny"—told me, "and you're wrong about that, Herb. You're just looking, but I already found."

"Like the Jesus folks or the est people, you found."

"Isn't your heart broken like everyone's?" she asked. "Have I touched a nerve? Don't you feel the need to seek and find?"

When I told Virgil about this conversation, he commented

with unusual succinctness, "She's right. I believe so."

Sometimes I like to dream of living with a wife and our kids in the country, where we might swim in a pond that has schools of minnows swiftly changing directions together when we dip a toe in. Actually, of course, I prefer the city, and taking my sons by my former wife to swim in the Press Club pool, and taking my daughter to dinner at Salmagundi (soup and salad) or David's (bagels and lox) after her acting class. And when the kids are not around, I like to try to figure out some of the destiny of humankind by figuring out what this carnival, Tivoli, toy town is all about. The minnows are dashing up and down. *I can relate to that,* people are saying.

Virgil is one friendly neighbor I have problems relating to. He is smart, educated, cheerful, and often covered with bruises. He is Group Chairman of the Jungian Men's Liberation Study group; that is, first among equals in a problem-solving committee inspired by the worker's communes of Chinese factories. No one has pointed out that the problems here are different from those in Chinese rural factories; in San Francisco, the People are worried about premature ejaculation, the limits of leather, and intestinal flora. The Masses do drugs and alcohol. Virgil is also Founding Director of the Gay Moralist's Union, director of the Campus Venereal Disease Holistic Club, Librarian for the Congregationalists for Victory Over Sexism Summer Seminars, and an occasional weekend caterer (he likes to cook). He earns a pretty good income out of doing good; he is an engaging individual entrepreneur; and since his only child was adopted by a tape music composer in Dallas whom his only wife married, he suffers little external drain on his energy or funds. Only living. Living itself is a drain on energy and funding.

That's a cherished goal, say those out in the Avenues, the San Francisco which is more like the old America of those who don't say, *I can relate to that.* Virgil, with all his quirks, represents something general and cautionary in this enormous village culture of alternative life-styles.

Can you relate to an instance of love in the manner of Virgil, if not granting it as a long-term cherished goal? A few days ago I heard a commotion, looked out my window, and noticed Virgil chasing a man with a suitcase. "You can't, you can't, you just *can't* leave now!" cried Virgil.

The man was his houseguest. He had stayed several weeks. He was a sturdy person who gave one a nostalgic feeling for the actors in fifties beach-party movies, only grown up to a bit of fleshiness. Sweating under the arms, lugging his suitcase, he was pursued by Virgil up the Broadway steps rather than into the Malibu surf. Virgil caught up with him. Virgil was trying to convince him of something. Virgil tugged at the suitcase, tugged at the man. The man shrugged smaller Virgil away. "You can't!" cried Virgil. Virgil pounced again, speedy on his little feet, crying out *You Can't!* with a deep howl of pain, chagrin, insult, pride, jealousy, love. Again the man pushed and hurried, handicapped by his stained, latch-sprung Goodwill suitcase. Virgil seized his arm.

In a mighty sweep of exasperation, the man slapped Virgil down and away. Virgil fell to the sidewalk. Virgil screamed. From the window I saw his arm bent like a bird's wing. I ran downstairs. The man was bending over him and saying, "Oh dear, oh dear."

Suddenly Virgil's voice was crisp and British, cool and knowledgeable and slightly supercilious, his eyes averted from the splinters of bone coming through at his broken elbow. "I think you had better transport me to Hospital," he said to me. "Not him, *you.* Or perhaps you had better call the ambulance service."

"Oh dear, what should I do?" asked the departing houseguest.

"I think you have done quite enough, my sweet," said Virgil. "I think you may leave and take your dirty laundry out of my life, Chris."

"Oh, how awful!" said the sturdy ex-houseguest.

I ran upstairs and called the ambulance and then hurried down again.

"You may go now, please," Virgil was telling his friend, who hung about in despair, making little circling reconnoitering maneuvers around his friend sprawled on the hilly steps of Broadway above the tunnel on Russian Hill. "I am going to Hospital soon, Chris. You had better go now or there will be questions. The Constable will be asking questions, Chris. Please leave me."

Chris accepted this invitation.

I stood waiting for the ambulance while Virgil smiled at me from below, his twisted arm seeming to flutter a little, like a broken wing. "It seems," he said, "it does no good for certain people to avoid doing their drinking in Samoan bars."

15
Maxifamily Doings in San Francisco

In San Francisco, most marriages seem to be in escrow, most relationships in a state of sustained title search. Out in the avenues, in the unexplored areas of San Francisco which are Middle American, marriage has about the same success and failure rate as everywhere else—which is not too good. But the new stuff is what we're talking about here.

For when former San Francisco Supervisor Dan White patted his gun into his belt, crawled through a window of City Hall and shot Mayor George Moscone, a sweet-tempered liberal, and Harvey Milk, the first officially gay supervisor—who once told me his constituency was "the fourteen-year-old runaway from San Antonio"—it was easy to say that poor Dan was driven mad by the frustrations of trying to live in a world he never made. Here he was—former policeman, fireman, aspiring conservative politician, family man—but what was happening to his city? Perhaps he wasn't really supposed to make his world anymore; perhaps he was supposed to try to get along, like everyone else. In the school my children attend, most students are the children of divorce by the time they reach the third grade. By the time they reach the eighth grade, they have been sorted out as the dependents of remarriages, re-remarriages, permanent single-parent households headed by harried women or harried men, or a number of even more experimental arrangements, such as communal agglomerations of lesbian mothers and homosexual fathers, tribes far gentler than the Apaches of Wild West legend.

My housecleaner is not an individual but a "family"—members of the Kerista commune, a group of young people who believe in "polyfidelity." That is, all the men and women are married to all the others, though I believe only heterosexually. Adultery consists in having sex with someone outside the group and they are quite firm about the immorality of violating the holy rules of their group puritanism. They are pretty good with the mop and the dishcloth, too, and prompt about their duties, but I'm never sure which one or ones will show up to vacuum my bachelor pad at the top of Russian Hill.

Several neighborhoods of San Francisco—the Polk area, known as Polkstrasse; the Castro-Noe Valley area, known as the Swish Alps—are clearly and interestingly governed by their homosexual communities. Other areas—North Beach, Clement Street, Potrero Hill, South-of-Market, the revived Haight—are also given part of their special flavor by large gay populations. In fact, as is widely suspected, San Francisco probably has the largest percentage of homosexuals of any city in the world—perhaps as much as twenty percent of the adult population. The industries of charm and pleasant consumption are multiplied by this world, which is not preoccupied with child support; those of us in the child-support business benefit by vacationing in their restaurants, shops, places of entertainment, and general resort culture.

A familiar cliché has it that the Western tilt casts all the loose nuts of America into California, which then divide into those who don't mind the freeways, who go to Los Angeles, and those who prefer not to drive so much, who come to San Francisco. It's possible to view this with consternation—the number of alcoholics, outpatients, psychopaths; the extremes of freedom-loving and the extremes of evasion of responsibility—and the afflicted can feel the same way. I once stood gossiping on Broadway in North Beach with some young advanced thinkers in full advanced-thinking hippie drag when one suddenly looked up and remarked: "Interracial couples are staring at *us.*"

These days, the sociological furnishings are more baroque. A recently divorced, attractive young woman friend of mine now works in a massage parlor to finance her graduate studies in social psychology. "I'm not a slave to big tips, my needs are modest, I don't do sexual massage," she says indignantly, "unless the vibes are right." Occasionally, of course, the vibes are right, and lately she reported that she rode with the flow with a twenty-three-year-old computer programmer and a seventy-some-year-old retired Chinese businessman ("he likes to kid around a lot"). The parlor where she works is not a refuge for cautious hookers-in-training; it's an established institution in a conservative neighborhood, ten years old, clean, well-hung with ferns, "homey," she tells me. It doesn't make the demands for performance that a brothel would make. It is relaxing for both client and masseuse. Some visitors only want, of course, a bit of conversation or the relief that Vick's won't give sore muscles.

All in all, it is just another contribution of the San Francisco counterculture to the well-being of a typical American neighborhood. My friend sees herself as much like a stewardess, a waitress, or a social worker—helping make men comfortable in a naughty, noisy, and confused world.

The body of marriage, that object once seen as holy, is

having vivisection performed on it these days; and nowhere in America is this complex surgery and transformation more evident than in the City and County of San Francisco. No wonder the bloom has come off America's affair with a lovely place. If San Francisco is the future, it is an ambiguous one. Do we still want to leave our hearts there?

Anyone in touch with children and with the recently unmarried knows that conjugal bankruptcy must provide the major resource of grief in America today. If we include the evident ache and loneliness of the quest for an "other"—the singles bars, the groups, the tattered remnants of the dating machine—we find a preoccupation comparable to the classic pains of the metaphysically lost. It's especially visible in the streets of San Francisco. The traditional alternative to loneliness, marriage, has proven to be painful for most Americans elsewhere, too.

In this no-win history, San Francisco, during a decade of highly visible chagrin following flower-child euphoria, now seems to be working something out that just might point to a manageable future. Perhaps the idealistic polyfidelity of Kerista is a symptom. It's easy to deplore and view with alarm and complain about kooks, but despite its troubles, San Francisco seems to become more and more interesting and, strange to say, more and more adjusted to its new maxifamily structure. The breakdown of the family and the consequent appearance of hordes of lonely crusaders has turned the city into a Tivoli of small, sweet restaurants, coffee houses, little theaters, poetry readings, neighborhood art and culture and salvation centers, groupy gardens. Civilized street loitering is practiced more diligently here than in any city in America. Without hearth and home, people tend to go out for coffee.

In a time of economic stress, the city stays alive. Whole neighborhoods are being revived thanks to the energies of the isolated. New conflicts occur, of course: Blacks are not happy to have their housing prettified by gay landlords who paint, plant, repair—and raise the rents. An unassimilated float of Chinese immigrants, some with money, are breaking up the old Italian community of North Beach and are changing the traditional, working-class, Catholic neighborhood of the Richmond District. Ethnic groups seem to provide the last bastion of traditional family structure, but the children of the Italians and Irish, of the Japanese, even of the Chinese, are learning to be footloose and fancy free.

The interesting thing about all this is not the muggings, the car aerials ripped off, the tragic murders and suicides and pathetic breakdowns. Nor is the backlash from the Middle American sections of town so new, even a backlash that lets Dan White off with a "voluntary manslaughter" conviction—which describes death brought without malice—after two murders carefully performed because he was "very angry" and had eaten a lot of Twinkies.

These things are familiar and engage the attention, of course, but the rest of the picture is fascinating and little known. The social price of change is extreme. For years most people assumed that the only way to rescue the matter was to go back to loyal marriage and family. Despite this good advice, it hasn't happened.

Finally, there are now some signs of success in the new patterns of city life emerging. Gay men and women, ardent feminists, businessmen who have taken up marathon running instead of marathon marriage, families of street people, families of searchers and questers, Zennies and filmmakers, a surprising mass acceptance of the necessity to find social sanction abroad, in the bosom of the city, rather than in the bosom of the nuclear family, give San Francisco some of its nervy charm. The city is being transformed, and the debris of transformation becomes famous. Tradition begins to give sanction to new habits.

What should be noted amid all the alarm-crying is that the city still works, and that in any case it may be one of the models for replacing the cities in which we grew up. (The other model is probably Los Angeles, the first experimental space colony on earth.)

When I revisit Cleveland, my old home town, I find a mini-San Francisco in its Coventry area, and in Memphis, Miami, San Antonio—in fact, in every major city in America—something of this style has given color and vitality to traditional places. Street life is allowed—strolling and letting the day or evening happen. Perhaps partly because of this change in concept, I am no longer arrested on what amounts to a charge of pedestrian behavior when I go walking in Beverly Hills.

When the family is evaporating all over America, San Francisco still may have something to teach by its painful, fun-filled example. Now in the 1980s, after the Viet Nam War and psychedelic drugs have passed into history and sexual freedom is a battle won, perhaps over-won, it sometimes seems that San Francisco has nothing more to do than to provide a colorful place for unattached people to compare the virtues of espresso with those of cappuccino.

"I'm spending this year on the outside," the recently divorced wife of a psychiatrist told me when I met her on three successive nights, browsing in City Lights Books, then at Just Desserts, then running on the Marina Green. "I've got to learn to get along with lots of folks and things," she said. "I'm not a wife anymore—I'm something else."

She and this city are running to find out what that something else might be.

16
Hi! Sex Is Not Located Only in the Head!

"Hi! I'm a journalist with a contract for a book on Men's Liberation, and I wonder if my tape recorder, my probing questions, and me personally could pay you the teensiest little in-depth visit . . ."

Resisting and postponing this teensy session of in-depthness, I finally agreed to meet the probing journalist, partly out of fraternal feeling for another writer's desire to do his job and partly for the opportunity to express my doubts about a contemporary idea—that men are not capable of true intimacy, only of palship, bowling together, business collaboration, barroom heartiness. The notion that men are cloned and without soul is political fume off the extremes of the women's movement, a seventies version of a received idea of the sixties—that white people don't know how to dance or dress up. Some of us don't, but some of us do. Some men are distant and isolated from their feelings, and some are not.

"Well, here I am at last!" He is a sensitive young man, this journalist, and he was wearing a filmy Indian shirt, the conventional Izro hairdo, a nice smile; I'll call him Matthew. He fussed with his electronic equipment and we settled down to coffee and largetalk. I explained (wait for the light; is it working?) that I have some longtime male friends; that we share the problems of our lives, support and help each other, laugh together, are silent together, mourn together; that if intimacy means this close trust and concern and pleasure in each other's company, I am intimate with them. The fact that we don't have sex together relieves us of some of the normal hazards of intimacy between men and women. For example, I am somewhat jealous and possessive of a woman, and usually she is of me. But my male friends have other close friends, they have lovers, I am only pleased for them. These old friendships grow intense, diminish, become intense again, as lives shift and alter, usually without the sad fading or desperate crack-ups of love affairs.

Matthew listened intently. I thought myself correct and convincing. I was busy communicating person-to-person despite the recording tape and the microphone. I could see Matthew squirming with a question and I paused. He asked: "Well, these male friends. Do you kiss them on the lips?"

I wasted tape. I looked at him in silence for a moment. The spool spun. Finally I said, "You haven't understood a word."

"No, no, I understand," he said, "really."

"Are you gay?" I asked.

"No, no, no, though I wish I could be freer, but I miss my wife—she's on a women's commune in Maine with our daughter—I really miss those little guys . . . *But do you?*"

"Those little guys are a woman and your daughter."

"I know, I know, it's just an expression. But if I'm not too upfront—*do you?*"

This soldier of androgyny, in his Indian shirt of blue and white gauze, was preaching a gospel of loving everyone, man and woman, with the same kisses on the lips, hugs, strokings, googoo murmurs, baby vocabulary. Is it comfort? Is it courtship? Is it consolation for the human destiny? No, for him it all came down to a challenge: If you're not an ideologically pure, indiscriminately erotic, big-time universal lover, you're a reactionary. You're backward. You're fast sliding out of fashion, so before it's too late, won't you please kiss me on the lips, huh? I'm not gay, but baby baby baby, won't you please? "Well, it's complicated," he said. "Some changes are coming down. My wife in Maine with our little guy, growing their own, I got to admit they're way ahead of us. I'm doing my best, exploring, seeking."

This willowy young man was in torment for the ideal of androgyny. And yet, I believe, in another time he would have been a reasonably contented husband and devoted father, spending this same devotion to a cause on the problem of unionization or pacifism or social justice. "I hope you'll listen to my outflow," he said, "although it's your input I really need. My wife and those guys, we're only separated, it's so far ahead of me it's—whew!"

The sigh was ineffable, like the thought. He wanted to be independent and do what was right. What was right was what he was told to do by the ideologues he had adopted, the latest herd of independent minds. They and he thought he should find men to make love to. He was undergoing heterosexual panic: the fear that he might be exclusively interested in the opposite sex. I remembered my own distress as a graduate student over the attentions of an academic adviser—his hand on my knee, his eye on my eye, his invitations to tea at his apartment. I feared this complication that Matthew sought.

"Matt, listen," I said pleadingly, "can't we leave what we do about our desires to appetite—what we really *want* we should want—and not to moral coding? Do you have to be contemporary even about what you simply like? Would you eat quiche just because it's the 'in' chow? Are you a smaller person for cutting off a few billion people from your sexual attention, while a few billion others are still in line?"

"Huh?" he asked. "You see it in such terms? I mean, you believe in exclusion?"

The question sent me into further spasms of explanation. Pedantry is probably not the proper answer to the his-lips-on-his-lips controversy, but there is no simple answer. I persisted. Yes, maybe Greeks and Arabs and some Polynesians sometimes do it. Maybe Anthony Quinn does it in every third movie. No, I don't think it's *wrong*. But I'm an American, raised in Lakewood, Ohio, and maybe not everything is as it should be in Lakewood, Ohio, and perhaps I've grown a little looser in my habits since living a number of years and passing my time in San Francisco, but still—I don't want to kiss my male friends on the lips. Appetite is not something to be legislated by theories, even modern ones about the moral necessity of androgyny to produce world peace and understanding.

I don't want to kiss some women, either. I want to kiss whom I want to kiss. I'll kiss my children on the lips, my sons, too, because I want to. There is no need, in this peculiar contemporary tantrum of *I want love, I want to be a theoretical lover,* to make love with everyone. Appetite involves choice, in food, in religion, in nationality, in profession, and in sexuality and love. Appetite doesn't even have to be rational; it may be a necessary escape from rationality.

Furthermore, perhaps there is truth in the old idea that opposites attract. I dearly hope and pray the scraping of my beard might please some woman now and then. But the scraping of my friend's beard against my beard does not entice me. There is even an economic advantage in sexual deliberation and exclusiveness. It means we can get on with it with the ones we like, and tend to business and other matters the rest of the time. But if every person I meet is a potential lover, I become one pitifully busy fella; more like a politician running a campaign than a lover. Decisiveness of sexual choice means we can concentrate passion and energy without lingering in nostalgia for some unremembered, perfect, amoebic union with all the other lost lonely guys.

Matthew's eyes were growing wide with this flood of reactionary emotion. He expected so much better of me. He was willing to listen, however; he was no Moonie. He let the tape run. He concentrated on his body language of rebellion and resistance, crossed arms, tapping foot, shallow breathing.

Androgyny, in fact, as we know from regarding the unisexual type, is finally antisexual. It is cuddling and being cuddled raised to the supreme power. I admitted to a liking for being cuddled and comforted, for cuddling and comforting—these are precious times in a life—but if a cuddle goes on forever it definitely causes cramps and claustrophobia. A life of constant morbid prying intimacy and sexual "openness" is a life fashionably unlived. It is a tantrum of no-delay nirvana. Choosing someone to love (even if he/she changes now and then, alas) is a way of coming out of the box of the Oedipus complex into the larger world. Hamlet would be much less interesting if the play consisted of only the closet scene.

"You're trying to be hard, Herb," said Matthew. "But I can see you're not really that kind."

"Pringle potato-chip goofy crunchy lovey love," I said.

"Doesn't do any good to be a sarcastic guy," he said. "I see beyond all of that."

Nice, isn't it? Keeps you coming back for more?

"Matthew, my friend," I said, "let tolerance rule. It's the moral imperative in your thesis that I dislike." May I now summarize? Let those who are homosexual do their thing. If there are any true bisexuals, let them keep busy. And for the rest, we can be content with only the necessary number of the opposite sex. It still gives lots of opportunity for choice, play, and adventure. And let us exercise our originality out of our own impulses and needs, history and metabolism, not out of the lecturing and hectoring of the visionaries of head-sex.

Matthew packed up his tapes and, as a testimony of respect for my dumb point of view, hugged me good-bye. We may never meet again, but we can both report a warm and meaningful encounter. He will write his book about the struggle for men to be friends, and loyally he will report that I am hostile to same-sex lip-kissing except with my father and my sons.

I try not to be uncool about this, but only to do what feels natural. Mouth-to-mouth resuscitation is appropriate under certain circumstances.

Nevertheless, I treasure my male friends. I hope Matthew finds some too, and doesn't feel obliged to make advances beyond what the traffic will bear. Some forms of intimacy don't require the blending of the mucous membranes. We even learn from sad history that the symbolic power of sexual union, no matter how intense when it occurs, gives no lifetime warranty of continued intimacy, chassis repair, and part replacement.

May you make distinctions, dear Matthew, and may your sex involve your whole body, not just the head.

17
Blind, Blind Date

"I'm not used to blind dates," I said. My good city acquaintance Merrill was telephoning an offer to fill an evening and perhaps, whoever knows? the rest of my life. "She's a folk-rock singer," he said. "Hasn't found the right group yet."

"Blind dates, that's kid stuff," I said.

"So that it shouldn't be blind, my dear friend, let me tell you. A folk-rock singer, part-time professional, good voice, great guitar, plus speed typist—a hundred and ten accurate words per minute, very much in demand as a temporary legal secretary. Plus she's been burning—well, why should I seek to flatter you?—*burning* very much to meet you."

"Uh. If she's got those talents—"

"Plus a high I.Q. Reads everything. Keen logical mind."

"—then what does she look like? how old?"

"Looks good to me. Tall, nice. Haha, you want to know what she smells like, too, my dear friend? You are really into caution and curriculum vitae, aren't you? Clean. Hahaha. Thirtyish."

"Ish?"

"Maybe latish. But lovely skin, graceful. Look! Don't hassle me. Very nice, my friend. Come to dinner."

Okay, though my good acquaintance Merrill probably was not the ideal judge of my needs in a blind date—true love forever plus a lot of fun—I could pass an evening with him and his friend Brad and this lady. "Her name?"

"Louisa."

A nice slightly old-fashioned semipro folk-rock speed-typist sweet-smelling high I.Q. sort of name. And Merrill was said, by himself and others, to be a gourmet cook. And he deeply desired that I share his pleasure in the new Twin Peaks manse he and Brad had taken to celebrate their seven glorious, trouble-filled, problem-solving years together. They had hacked it. The itch for change was eased by a new house hooked up with advanced equipment for sound transmission and ethnic cooking. I could use some 32-track Berlioz. Even in my wan state, I could use some wok-seared vegetables with unbruised health, vitamins, and good intentions.

My hair had actually been wet with water, as I used to do on my blind or at least nearsighted dates in Lakewood, Ohio, so many years ago. While we waited for Louisa, Merrill and Brad showed me the house, upstairs, downstairs, garage, closets. I sniffed the air with appreciation, but there were no signs of cooking. "I decided to take us out to this little bistro in Mill Valley," said Merrill. "I want you to try my new Caddy Eldorado, too. We'll have drinks here first. Louisa hasn't seen the house since we finished the kitchen."

The doorbell tolled its Swiss melody, electronically amplified throughout. Merrill ran to greet Louisa, calling behind him, "We had the bell hooked into the stereo."

A nice touch, I mentioned to Brad. Brad said, "He's taking her bag. She's hanging up her coat." Then Louisa entered and shook my hand and blushed. Unusually nice, smooth delicate skin and unusually large hands and feet. Somehow I knew at once—the truth came to me!—and was thinking with inelegant panic. A restaurant in Mill Valley where my former wife will surely walk in with some sterling chap. "Why, both of you are blushing!" Brad cried. His voice echoed from formica beams in the lodge ceiling. "You'd think they never had a blind date before. But that's how Merrill and I met, seven years ago, and not even through good friends."

"Through an advertisement in a laundromat," Merrill said, squeezing his hand, "and weren't we both embarrassed? But we got over it."

"You're working on it," Louisa said, laughing a delighted little trill. She winked at me, the first of many winks.

This little Provençale bistro in Mill Valley was layered with warm and friendly aromas of onion, tomatoes, peppers, eggplant, and perhaps a soupçon of garlic. It used to be a Porsche garage before it got to be a traditional Provençale bistro, Merrill told me; he knew the owner, who greeted us with ecstasy, with raised pencil, with a round of drinks on the house. Brad suggested, motion seconded by me, made unanimous by Louisa, that Merrill order for all of us.

He put on his other glasses. "Food, food," he murmured. "Let's see the wine card first. I don't think a French tonight, strange as that may seem; a California. I've really gone bananas over the great Californias since I sold my condo and purchased my home." After careful reading he slipped off his other glasses while the steward waited, slid them into the breast pocket of his suede jacket, and put on his original glasses to tell the steward what we wanted.

"Excellent, outstanding choice," the steward murmured, rubbed himself, made himself vanish.

Merrill smiled and clapped his hands. He took off his glasses again and put them in a different pocket. He gazed at Louisa and me through naked eyes, frankly pouched with difficult living. Merrill was a large, bearded, hearty, booming-voiced man with a delighted smile growing delighteder as he beamed upon us. "Ah, good friends," he said.

The wine arrived, was tasted, was good if not great, was offered in clicks to friendship.

May I now skip the food, trusted reader? There were garlic, peppers, and sauces, aubergine, veal, and chilled salads, nothing wrong with the food; there was a duck with orange sauce for Louisa. But this is not a gourmet story. This is a story about hope, faith, charity, and the lack of charity. "When I joined the church and had my operation," Louisa said.

"Which church?"

"Roman Rite."

"Which operation?"

She blinked at me, her heavy mascara shredded on her eyelids. Well, she had brought up church and operation. "I don't keep secrets from my friends," she said. "They're like family, closer sometimes. I lubricate. I'm normal in every way." She gazed demurely at my lap. She touched my elbow. I was eating. It was the touch on the elbow of a person making a political or literary point, or of a relative, or of a normally insistent believer. My eating was the eating of a skeptic or of someone in a state of unease for whom eating is a demonstration that life will go on, no matter what life does to itself.

"I lubricate normally," she said. "I find you very intelligent."

"He has a wonderful, keen sense of humor of his own," said Merrill of me, as if I were a visiting Japanese, "but you have to learn to dig his form of levity."

Merrill blessed us all. He had an old-fashioned brown mole athwart his cheek, with three irregular-sized ash-colored hairs growing from it. In California they change such things by removing them. It looked like a badge of some rare genetic distinction. I didn't really want him to praise me. Louisa's gaze into my lap, where a red napkin lay like a limp shield, was demure but insistent—it was a look of heavyweight wistfulness.

One can be encouraged in adversity. I realized, thanks to Merrill's praise, that my sense of humor might be on trial. I should rise to the vision of my former wife coming in with a heck of a young man and finding me crowded into this cozy booth with Merrill, Brad, and large-featured Louisa. I was ready for the test; the fear was now declared defunct. But I sincerely hoped it would be heeded.

"Are you Jewish?" Louisa asked. "Because the name, you're quite attractive and all, but the name—"

"Yes. Are you?"

"My parents, true," she said. "Me, not. I hope this doesn't hurt your feelings."

"It's foolish to judge others," I said. "But I have a tendency toward foolish. Are you running away from something?"

"Oh dears," said plural-minded Brad. "Like yourself. We're all super people."

"I lubricate normally," Louisa said.

"I only learned I'm soopah recently in my group, but I really learned it. Now I know everybody is soopah," said Brad. "Even if you didn't lubricate, what's wrong with a little K-Y jelly?"

"But I do!"

"That's reasonable," Merrill said.

"Reasonable?" Louisa demanded angrily. "Cost me eight thousand dollars for my birthright, and that's reasonable? Do you think Medicare would handle it? God, I had a fight on my hands from beginning to end."

I said soothingly, "I had a daughter in an incubator for a

month. And twin sons all at once, too. Everything costs."

"I had to go to Stanford Medical Center, the doctors there. My shrink here said there was no doubt I was a woman where it counts, in the soul. Also I had something like a woman's bladder to begin with already. You could build from those. I said to those docs in Palo Alto: I demand to lubricate! Fuck the expense, excuse my passion, I'm young and horny, I want to be perfect."

"You look good." This is the comment one cannot help making under such circumstances if one has any responsibility to the needs of others. I have such.

"No beard," Louisa said. "Smooth. Here, feel." Her paw seized mine and guided it. Smooth chin. "My shrink discharged me. Said I'm normal, bladder, the works, anybody in his right mind knows that."

Nevertheless, I felt like arguing certain points. "Not normal," I said, "not to be Jewish if you're born one."

"Try the cold zucchini vinaigrette," said Merrill. "Here, you haven't sampled it, so how can you know?"

"Yes, yes," said Louisa. Her look of scorn said: *What's important? I spit on K-Y jelly.*

I was all this old, with five children, unmarried again, and brought to this single swing in a Mill Valley Provençale former Porsche garage with ferns and a headwaiter talking about his back trouble. "An old badminton injury," he said. "Plus I twist sometimes in my sleep and wake myself up. If someone happens to be with me, they say, 'Stop twisting.'"

"Have I got a doctor for you," said Merrill. "He studied chiropractic and nutrition with a Korean master in Seattle."

"Personally, with all due respect to Merrill, whom I respect as a person to a maestro, I'd join a group," Brad said. "So many of these things go away if you have a really caring, nurturing relationship or ships—"

Louisa was drumming her fingertip or tips on the table. We had gotten off the subject.

"—in an upfront and caring group. You should have been there when we all wrote postcards to Florida orange juice."

A vigorous smell of healthy flesh, busy with its metabolism, arose from Louisa's shoulders. This is a smell, like a tropical courtyard in the first flush of thunderstorm, sheets of feeling pelting the earth, which I loved in the Midwest, in France, in Haiti; and now should politely learn to love off Louisa's perfumed arms, although there was also a back-alley scent of anxious mobilization. I didn't love it yet.

"One thing I thought before isn't true now," Louisa said. "It's still hard to find a man who's not hung-up. The really twisted ones, I mean dumb kinks, should do what I did, but instead they—" She stopped and gazed at me.

Yes, some dumb kinks dream of sweet girls who welcome without demanding, without sleek back-alley anxieties; whose gaze is equal, kind, and inciting; who take pride in what she is and in what he might be. Louisa had evolved to a new level. She had radically abolished her circumcision; she no longer dreamed from memories; she wanted a purer invention. "So are you a finder or a seeker?" she asked me.

"I don't know. Those are categories."

Merrill, mighty, bearded, high-colored in the cheek, looked happy at the serious conversation of serious people. Brad looked bored at this turn from interesting conversation, but did his best to arouse his own interest. "I'm both a finder and a seeker. I'm me."

Merrill's laughter boomed out. "I don't have to look; I found it. If you're ready in your heart, you can find it in a *Spectator* ad: 'Adventurous Male Likes It Every Day. No kooks.'"

"You're kook enough for both of us. You're just a hunk of kook," Brad fondly stated.

"It's stood the test of time," Merrill said.
"You see, you see, you see?" Louisa demanded of me.
"You have to allow me my own way," I said.
"Of course, of course, of course," said Merrill.
"Really," said Brad.
"So long as you're not a pothole, what I call," said Louisa.
"I'll strive not to be."
"Whatever's right," said Merrill. "Louisa, you said you had high hopes."
"Oh, not without reason." She lowered her eyes. "There is so little time in life, our hours must be festivals. So I got this friend in the Auto License Bureau. How could I spend this soiree with you if you were, I don't know, a pothole, a Capricorn? Please forgive me, dear. He told me birthdate, color of eyes, hair, violations. Forgive, okay? There's only so many soirees in the week."
"I feel the same way."
"I like you. I thought I'd just throw that out," Louisa said.
"Thank you."
She steadily tossed zucchinis from her plate to her mouth with the fork as intercom, and steadily she continued this forward march of her liking. "Today I'm happy with my body. Meeting you, I'm happy with my bod. I thought I'd just throw that out."
"Thank you again."
"My feet were killing me—those new heels. But I feel fine now. Good food, good conversation, good company." Brad and Merrill were hushed and watchful as I said thank you. "Oh, I know you've had your full share of midnight tears. I thought I'd just throw that out."
I believed I could believe her, since she already had thrown out so many things—her history, her jockey shorts—and somehow also had trashed her circumcision in the process, converting the trembling and unsure instrument into

a steelbeltradial, industrial-duty receptacle which becomes moist on demand. The buck stopped here. She thought she wouldn't just throw this out.

We drank more California. We nibbled at crusts of sourdough French bread. We had perfect little cups of espresso with little twists of lemon in them. Louisa bit her lemon rind with her front teeth, staring at me, to release the flavor.

I should have been carrying in my sleepy sons from the car after a day in the sun. I should be helping my daughter with her French. I should be writing to my old parents. Instead, past the middle of my life, I was having a blind date with a Taurean hairdresser, an aerospace engineer who knew what he liked, and a lady who was like a new foreign sportscar, with a superlative sealed system, self-lubricating. She touched my arm. I longed for my sweaty, squirming, sleepy sons.

"Some people," Louisa was saying, "you kiss, and you get that tingle. You know what I mean? That tingle? Well, my friend in the Auto License Bureau—I was telling you, I don't get that tingle. But I do get birthdate, color of eyes, height, weight, age, and I can tell if you're a hunky guy. And sometimes, Herb, you can use truth better than a tingle."

"I know what you mean," I said. Calm. Life must be a festival. My children were asleep by now, anyway.

"You're warming up," Louisa said, and guided my hand to touch her chin and cheek. They were smooth, no growth at all. Not silky, but definitely in the range of Smooth.

"It's the wine," I said cheerfully, breaking contact of hand and cheek, "plus I feel good. I'm not having the glooms like sometimes. I just feel good and we can let it go at that."

"It makes me truly happy."

And so I would just smile if my former wife walked in with some fine fellow, easy and comfortable; she would smile back and wave. I could get up early next morning, suggest taking the kids to the House of Pancakes. Soon my sons would be too big to carry, but I still liked to carry them. In the evening, sleepy, they liked it, but in the morning they would dash shrieking over the hot asphalt of the House of Pancakes parking lot—French toast, waffles, or blueberry pancakes, plus ice cream, plus syrup down their t-shirts.

Merrill beamed. He was mighty and broad-shouldered and kept his mole. Brad batted his eyes at Merrill, their evening's work done. A smell in my nostrils like a wet, extinguished fireplace.

"So let's go," said Merrill. "Did you really love the duck in orange sauce?"

"We liked the pecan roll, didn't we, Herb?" Louisa said. "And the wine was really *à la carte.*"

As we swung satiated out of the Provençale Porsche garage, good-byes from the badminton-playing head-waiter, good-byes all around, nice duck, nice duck, Louisa gaily took my arm. Not since long ago had I been a single; not since long ago had I enjoyed such a really boss, dynamite sinus headache. Feeling my arm stiffen, Louisa said: "I can't just do this all by myself cold turkey, Herb."

What's to become of the gray-bearded lad now?

Which might have been the end of this account. But Merrill telephoned the next day to talk about our evening. "You know, you understand surely, that Louisa hasn't many good friends in this world. She works the White Glove typing pool, but that's got to be temporary. You don't make good friends in the typing pool. She thought everything would be different, but there aren't many real persons around this world."

"I know. I'm sorry," I said.

"Not that you were anything but a gentleman."

"I understand."

"I don't really meddle. Brad always says that's not my way.

Ride with the flow is our rule. I had hopes for you two, but I suppose I should have told you first."

"I figured it out. It's okay."

"You did?"

"It was clear."

"It was? So lonely. And me so sad about it. Louisa is all alone now, and there should be such sweetness in life. I'm kind of distraught about her. She used to be, when she was a man, my wife."

18
The Post-Hip Generation

A young man called because he is doing an article about publishing first novels in San Francisco. "You mean writing them, don't you?" I asked.

"Oh, yeah. But the problem, bottom line, is how to make the contacts so you can publish it."

"No, sir. The problem, bottom line, is to make the contact so you can write it. There's only one contact you need to make."

I didn't want to have to tell him what that was. If he was a writer, he should be able to figure it out. Even by telephone I could tell he was thinking, and he turned kind of slow and thoughtful. Maybe he had interrupted my morning. He regretted this, if so. He wanted to gain my favor again. It was one of those sunny dry mornings in San Francisco, a wisp of fog over the bay, when a fellow considers whether to remember first love or have another cup of coffee. If the metabolism works right, you can do both at the same time. He asked: "Who's a good agent in San Francisco?"

Naturally I was relieved not to have to write my book, but instead I could be informational, helpful, irritated, and patronizing. All this pleases a man, although it leaves a bit of ego hangover. I talked to him about scouts, editors, magazines, small-press publishers. I assured him that one writes by writing, not by acquaintance; and if you're talking about novels, one publishes in the same way, by writing the book. Knowing people won't even save postage. Perhaps nonfiction is different, and you get a publisher by knowing someone, not by writing a book. But I doubt it.

The young man said he was writing an article. I suggested he was a bruised would-be, searching to squeeze some juice out of the rind of his rejection slips. He needed to know Why. You see, I am sorry enough for him to create a flowery, sentimental, slightly acid metaphor.

"It's difficult, I agree," I said. "First novels are printed, but many aren't. However, second and third and fifth novels also find trouble getting published, or distributed, or read. The problem is never solved, sir."

His silence now meant: why do you keep calling me sir?

"Man, I haven't got the answer," I said.

He was encouraged. "Could we get together and rap about writing?"

I smelled cigarettes, coffee, hamburgers and a slow exhalation of advice from me. The first smells were okay, but not the last. Who knows, I thought, if he were a pretty girl, I would be more indulgent. And so out of shame I said: "Sure, come up and I'll see what I can do for you. But I think I've told you everything."

And that was the sadness of it. All he wanted to know was how-to. I'm not sure I could tell him why, or what, or even show him the way to ask those questions. He was on his way and I was putting on the mask.

He arrived and I thought: nothing but agony here. He was

a thin, harassed, groovy kid, who had smoked a lot of grass (hair, teeth) and used a little cocaine or speed (skinny, spidery) on top of a lot of good California sun and food and middle-class parents (tall, big-boned). He reached out to take my hand. His was clean and dry, and the gesture meant to be respectful, I think. It left no fingerprints. I made instant coffee. We looked at the Transamerica building across Russian Hill and North Beach. "How old are you?" I asked.

He sighed. He put more sugar in and stirred and gazed at me.

We talked about life and love and the difficulty of finding a place in the world and the passion for literature and the dangers of success and failure. We drank more coffee, passed the coffee peak, and we talked some more about fate and desperation and responsibility and the youth of America.

"My men's group," he murmured, knowing he would have to confess to them as he now copped out to me. "My men's group thinks I'm still performance-oriented. I'm success-hungry. I can't relax, it's my hang-up from my parents. I want to get to the top. Why write for others? they ask me. We have a community right here. I can't answer that, but somehow, talking it all out in my men's group doesn't hack it for me."

"You're an artist and you can't look back," I said.

"Huh?"

"Bob Dylan song," I said.

"The book has two parts. Part One: My Lovers, Female. I call that Part the First. Part Two: My Lovers, Male. It's fictionalized, of course. Part the Second. I change all the names except maybe my own. Fischer-Hoffman Therapy helped me work it through, plus I got my Group, only they're not so supportive anymore since I had the thing Xeroxed and I'm sending it out. I'd like to sell it as well as finding the truth about myself and my lovers. I paid my dues, man. I want to live a little better. As an old pro, I thought you could advise."

"Thank you for that compliment."

His eyes burned into mine. We were making contact. He communicated. Communication was not the problem; it was what he communicated that troubled me. Nevertheless, in my own way, I sought to remain in touch.

"You like to visit our group one time?" he asked. "You wouldn't have to tell the truth the first time, just listen. I think you might could handle it, man."

You can come free of any charge, he was saying.

He pulled at the ends of his mustache. It was a well-tugged drop-out mustache. He knew that half of an I-Thou relationship involved listening, and so, humming softly, listened me out. And so, on the third cup of coffee I once more asked this skinny, nervous, anxious kid that first question which he had not yet answered: "How old are you?"

"Forty," he said.

19
The Rise of the People People

Ten years ago, returned from Biafra, I was describing a hospital filled with children dying of starvation, a disease for which food is the cure; before I left the hospital there was an air raid and I saw a huge, muscular man dying in the posture of crucifixion, screaming, muscles transfixed, a rocket having passed through his body. My visitors were a San Francisco psychiatrist and his wife. Perhaps I was preoccupied, maybe somewhat overwrought. The psychiatrist, I noticed, was working his hands impatiently as I talked. He looked at his wife, then at me, and then he said: "Why do you suppose you take this so personally, Herb?"

I threw him out of my house and he reported that I was a disturbed, distraught, "problematic" individual. I was and am "problematic," whatever that might mean.

This doctor referred everything in life, history, and human suffering to his own preoccupations: himself, his career, the management of feeling.

Enough of him.

Recently a young woman friend told me about her last

lover, a college dean. Early in their affair he broke into tears of love, lust, gratitude, hope; copious, streaming, salty tears. She was touched. Later it came to her notice that he cried rather frequently—a telephone call from her would elicit tears; a poem of Yeats; a minor annoyance from his ex-wife or ex-children. There was very little emotional distance between a mosquito itch and a wailing torrent. He was one of those who wept while waiting in line to see *Love Story*. Finally, before she gave him up, she said, "I don't understand this childishness, Dean." And he answered, sobbing, "You move me so much it's wonderful." He couldn't go on.

She couldn't go on, either.

What we have here is the sin of exclusive reference to Me, Myself, and I. What we have here is a preoccupation with honest, upfront, gut-level where-does-this-strike-*me*. A young woman I know, confronted by either disaster or joy, anything from mass murder-suicide in Guyana to a young happy couple enjoying their first child, asks: "I'm a people person, how do you *feel* about that, Herb?"

What we have here is the rise of the People People.

Coincidentally—certain clichés are instantaneous and spread like the flu—another person, the man I'll call Buffalo Bill, also confessed to being a People Person. But whom does this embrace include? Are the People People destined for greatness in the general sympathy line?

We have all been taught love as the means to fulfill ourselves. Next question: Have we overlearned the lesson? Without violating the pieties of the time, perhaps we need to study next how to regulate the predatory and programmatic forms of love which have become popular consumer products, like baroque music and mouth fresheners. Who can oppose Vivaldi, sweet exhalation, and tender concern?

Yet there remains the problem of how we mean them and

use them. I'm not ready to testify against love as devotion to someone or something, love as caring for others, love as compassion, love as desire. These old-fashioned occasions for tenderness and sacrifice of self are being endangered not only by neglect and failure—the familiar troubles—but also by artificial, formularized, prepackaged attention. The fast-food forms of love which really serve to look back only upon the lover himself or herself with adoration. The lovee is a convenience, an occasion for private bliss, like a tummy tv. Something icky has become a style of the age: a fully expressed, deeply explored, zoom-lens, saturation-bombing love. People-Person love. Predatory and programmatic love provides a technical boost to the pooped soul. HAVE YOU HUGGED YOUR BUMPER STICKER TODAY?

Every viewer-with-alarm in America can supply his own repertory of the tales of me-ness. Trampling us down like a slowly moving, inexorable line of disco dancers, the pop sociologists tell of our preoccupation with our own feelings; simultaneously, from another corner of the hall, the pop psychologists give instructions in how to listen to the message of our sincerest impulses, how to ride with the flow, how to win with Number One, or at least lose at the highest possible level. Viet Nam and race and poverty and even drugs were last decade's joys. The advanced protest for Now is that we were born into pain and loneliness: *poor us.* To find your way through the dark woods, follow these rules . . .

Of course, all this may seem to be only one more contemporary bad micro-mini manner. We really are still concerned with other matters, with justice, inflation, war, peace, our apparent summons from on high to behave like human beings, not animals. But I believe the matter is serious—serious enough for satire, serious enough to be hooted off the world's stage. We are studying to be our own best friends with an enthusiasm more proper to religious revival.

A few months ago I was sitting with a friend, a shy, intelligent, and gentle dying man. It was one of the last times we could go out together. He was in pain; he was doomed. But he was still insisting on enjoying while he could the pleasures of food, talk, and his connection with the living. He spoke about how he passed his time when he was not with the doctors. He was reminding us both about what still made life worthwhile: a morning without too much pain, a friendly wiggle from his dog, a letter from his daughter, a smile from his wife, the look of certain San Francisco skies, reading and writing. "I don't ask too much," he said. "But I get more than ever from those things. That's a plus. They are really there. I can even think about them when I don't feel so well."

He was smiling. I believe he felt a kind of happiness.

Just then, a commotion filled the little restaurant. A tall man with a Buffalo Bill mustache came pushing past the other eaters. "Hey, man, hey!" he cried. He was throbbing and emitting sparks. He seized the sick man by the shoulders and shook him. "Listen, I heard about it. I heard about you, brother, I just want to say up front I love you, what else can I say?"

My friend, afflicted with the jaundice, the emaciation, and the weakness of liver dysfunction, tried to turn in his chair to face the visitor. He was jerked around by a powerful hand. "I just plain love you," Buffalo Bill was saying, "and I'm all torn up inside. I want you to know you mean a heck of a lot in my life. I wish you'd have told me and I didn't have to hear it from others. You're just a perfect, helpful, caring individual, and I'm destroyed by the news."

The sick man squirmed in a frantic grip. "How've you been, Bill?" he asked.

Bill's face was working east and west with emotion, the mustache was wet from his eating, his entire being expressed a laughing and crying frank turmoil—the *communication* of turmoil. He said, "Oh perfect, perfect, as well as you can expect, I got over my breakup, the divorce is coming through okay, she gets the house and the car, shit, she can have it. I got my reality, my space. But listen: The important person right now is *you*. How're you taking *your* crisis?"

"I'm okay, Bill."

"Say, could we have lunch this week?"

"Well . . ."

"Listen, you can have lunch with this person—" The storm abated and I could be introduced. "—You can lunch with an old buddy like me, too. I mean, if you feel like it. I'm a people person, I try to understand what you're going through. I'm sure you got lots on your mind. I don't want to put any pressure on you. If it's right. You got to do whatever's right. You can say anything, you can just lay it all out to me. I don't want any punches pulled between us, pal. The thing is rotten. Your karma has always been truly one of the best, a really outstanding karma, and I just can't get it through my head." He pounded the side of his head symbolically, like a man with water in an ear. "Why you? Why *you?* But at a time like this, there's only one true answer—ride with the flow. That's what I did when my wife left me, and it felt right." He released our friend for a moment and put his hands on his belt. "I'm centered. The pain is gone like—" He blew an invisible bubble into the air. With a concerned but triumphant smile, he watched it sail away.

"I'm pleased for you, Bill."

"So you'll call, won't you? Everyone's been talking about you. All your pals are broken up, not just me personally. It's a rotten, rotten deal coming down, that's my frank opinion, so call. We all got to take responsibility. Lunch? Lunch? Lunch?"

And then, not knowing what to do next, what to say next, feeling all this emotion boiling up in him, Bill suddenly grabbed the sick man's cheeks and peered into his eyes and abruptly, impulsively, bent down and kissed him. Tears were rolling down Bill's cheeks. With one last pinch and squeeze, he turned and went back to his own table, ready to tell his lunch date about the interpersonal crisis he had just gone through, shaking his head and dabbing his face with a red Farmer John handkerchief.

We sat in silence for a moment. Then my friend winked at me and grinned. "I saw it coming. I was sure he was going to kiss me on the lips, but I managed to catch an updraft and he only got my chin." I said nothing. "He really means well, though."

"I can't judge that," I said, judging that.

"Well, he's had a difficult time."

"He looks prosperous," I said.

"He's okay."

I asked one more question before we returned to our former conversation. "What does he do?"

"Merchandiser," my friend said, echoing Buffalo Bill's rumble. "Developed his own mixture of Jungian and Gestalt therapy. He learned a lot from Werner. He gets people in touch with their real feelings."